MEXICO CITY

By John Cottrell
and the Editors of Time-Life Books

Photographs by Harald Sund

THE GREAT CITIES · TIME-LIFE BOOKS · AMSTERDAM

The Author: Born in Weston-super-Mare, England, John Cottrell entered journalism as a reporter on the *Bristol Evening Post* and later became a sports editor with Beaverbrook Newspapers in London. His first book, published in 1964, was *The World Stood Still*, a best-selling account of the assassination of President John F. Kennedy. He has also written biographies of contemporary figures including Muhammad Ali and Laurence Olivier. As a freelance writer, he has travelled extensively in North and Central America.

The Photographer: Harald Sund was born in Seattle, Washington, in 1943. After graduating from the University of Washington, he became a freelance photographer. His work has been published in books and magazines around the world. He was also the photographer for *Tokyo* in *The Great Cities* series.

TIME
LIFE
BOOKS

TIME-LIFE INTERNATIONAL
EUROPEAN EDITOR: Kit van Tulleken
Design Director: Louis Klein
Photography Director: Pamela Marke
Chief of Research: Vanessa Kramer
Text Director: Simon Rigge (acting)
Chief Designer: Graham Davis
Chief Sub-Editor: Ilse Gray

THE GREAT CITIES
Series Editor: Deborah Thompson
Editorial Staff for *Mexico City*
Designers: Derek Copsey, Joyce Mason
Picture Editors: Caroline Alcock, Frances Middlestorb
Staff Writers: Mike Brown, Anthony Masters
Text Researchers: Krystyna Davidson, Elizabeth Loving
Assistant Designer: Zaki Elia
Design Assistant: Elaine Maddex
Sub-Editor: Nicoletta Flessati
Editorial Assistant: Katie Lloyd

Editorial Production
Production Editor: Ellen Brush
Traffic Co-ordinators: Pat Boag, Joanne Holland
Picture Department: Catherine Lewes, Stephanie Lindsay, Belinda Stewart Cox
Art Department: Julia West
Editorial Department: Ajaib Singh Gill

The captions and the texts accompanying the photographs in this volume were prepared by the editors of TIME-LIFE Books.

Valuable assistance was given in the preparation of this volume by Bernard Diederich, TIME-LIFE News Service, Mexico City, and by Koos Siewers and Ida Novi Paniagua, TIME-LIFE Books, Mexico City.

Published by TIME-LIFE International (Nederland) B.V. Ottho Heldringstraat 5, Amsterdam 1018.

© 1979 TIME-LIFE International (Nederland) B.V. All rights reserved. First printing in English.
ISBN 7054 0500 1

Cover: A modern walkway creates an angular frame for the truncated remains of the Great Pyramid of Tlatelolco, one of the Aztecs' largest temples. In this area, now known as the Plaza of the Three Cultures, the last great battle between the Aztecs and their Spanish conquerors was fought in 1521.

First end paper: Rows of edible sugar skulls, each marked with a child's name, stare from a display on a confectionery stall. The skulls are bought for children on the Day of the Dead (November 2), a festival of remembrance that combines pagan and Christian elements.

Last end paper: At the abandoned, pre-Aztec temple complex of Teotihuacan, 30 miles from Mexico City, a group of visitors shrink to ant-like proportions as they stroll along a walkway traversing one sloping, stone-built face of the monumental Pyramid of the Sun.

Contents

I

Creation of Two Cultures

I should declare my personal feelings at the outset. They are curiously mixed: I adore Mexico City for its vibrant, sensual and supremely colourful qualities; but I also dislike the place for its many unarguably disturbing aspects. It has scarcely a single feature that I can view with indifference. Moreover, I know many Mexicans who regard the capital of their republic with the same kind of ambivalence. They complain endlessly about polluted air, traffic-clogged streets, unemployment, shortages of housing and water, corruption and pettifogging bureaucracy. Yet, most of them react with impassioned indignation to any outsider who expresses his own criticisms. The tendency to inspire conflicting emotions is one of Mexico City's most noticeable and deeply rooted characteristics.

It is the oldest continuously occupied city in the western hemisphere. It represents a fusion of two cultures. Originally named Tenochtitlan, it was founded in the 14th Century by the Mexica, one of several American Indian tribes known as Aztecs who inhabited the lofty, lacustrine valley of Anahuac, now called the Valley of Mexico. It grew amid the cluster of lakes into a city of Venetian splendour, capital of an Aztec empire that reached from the Atlantic to the Pacific coasts of central America.

Nearly 200 years later, Tenochtitlan was reduced to rubble by Hernán Cortés and his army of Spanish conquistadors. On the ruins of this great pagan civilization, they built Mexico City. Subsequently, the two disparate cultures—Mexican and Spanish—merged to such a degree that Mexico is now populated predominantly by a *mestizo* (mixed-blood) people. Arguably the joining of these two civilizations explains why opposing characteristics may be attributed to Mexico City, and to Mexicans in general.

Throughout the city, museums, buildings and monuments evoke the different periods of the brilliant and varied past. The spacious magnificence of the National Museum of Anthropology, in my view the most exciting museum in the world, provides a modernistic shrine to the nation's Indian inheritance. Colonial mansions, historic churches and public squares offer Spanish vistas of florid stone façades, glazed tiles and decorative ironwork. Then there are the open-air cafés, smart restaurants and expensive shops, the ballet, opera, theatres, concerts and art galleries, providing all the assets and luxuries to be expected of a thriving capital city that is the centre —political, industrial, cultural and intellectual—of a rapidly developing country, and one that is now confident in its possession of enormous oil reserves. If one also considers the glorious climate, the exuberance of a fiesta-loving people, the haunting quality of their traditional music and

Heavily polluted air—one of Mexico City's many persistent environmental problems— screens the rays of the evening sun, forming a red aura behind the slender silhouette of the 44-storey Latin American Tower. Built in 1956, it is the highest building in the centre of the city, offering an unrivalled view of the capital from its 42nd-floor observatory. It carries a television mast and a digital time display.

their stunning mestizo beauty, it is easy to see why anyone should fall in love with this wonderfully exhilarating city.

All that is hateful about Mexico City is as easily defined. The chief problem—or rather the root of many problems—is its sheer size. In recent decades, the city has become hopelessly overcrowded and unmanageable, spreading itself so far and fast in haphazard growth that it has quite outgrown the resources and services that are available to support it. If the whole conurbation of the metropolitan area—Mexico City proper and the surrounding sprawl of suburbs, satellites and shanty towns—is reckoned together, then Mexico City is the largest city in the world, out-stripping Shanghai, Tokyo or New York. According to the most recent statistics, it has more than 13 million inhabitants, covers at least 289 square miles, and is still growing at a rate that, if sustained, will take it to more than 32 million people by the year 2000—greater than the projected size of London, Paris and Rome combined.

The environmental problems of the city are greatly aggravated by its extraordinary position at the southern end of the Valley of Mexico, a shallow depression 35 miles long and 50 miles wide that lies more than 7,000 feet above sea-level and is flanked on three sides by mountains. Leaving aside arctic wastes, arid deserts and impenetrable jungles, it is difficult to imagine a more unfavourable site for a giant metropolis. Whereas almost every other great city is strategically placed either by the sea or on a major river, Mexico City is some 250 miles inland, almost equidistant from the Pacific Ocean to the west and the Gulf of Mexico to the east. Although conveniently central for communication by road, rail and air with the rest of the country, the city has no permanently flowing rivers to

A row of balconied houses three and four storeys high on Guatemala Street are among the few survivors of 19th-Century Mexico City's residential architecture. Such houses are now found only in the city's oldest, central quarter.

aid transportation or provide water for irrigation and industrial purposes. Standing on a volcanic belt, it is subject to frequent earth tremors, and its extreme altitude and mountainous approaches create special problems in bringing in water from outside the valley.

Over the centuries the lakes around the original city were progressively filled in to provide space for urban expansion. But the subsoil is still so spongy in those areas that some buildings have been sinking at a rate of a foot a year. Many have been distorted by uneven subsidence. The monumental Metropolitan Cathedral, for example, has a main floor that inclines upwards in some parts and downwards in others. I have seen two churches with walls leaning outwards and domes opened like oysters. The city's principal centre of culture—the sumptuous, white-marbled Palacio de Bellas Artes—has sunk eight feet since its completion in 1934.

A few decades ago, the evidence of subsidence was so alarming that engineers talked ominously of a day when the old city—now the eastern sector of central Mexico City—would sink to oblivion in a sea of mud. Some planners even advocated abandoning the capital altogether. Instead Mexican architects responded boldly to the challenge by constructing new high-rise structures on floating foundations, or on pilings driven into solid levels many feet below the surface. Ironically, during earth tremors, the unstable subsoil of the city proves an advantage, serving as a cushion against shocks and allowing the buildings, as one seismologist puts it, "to dance".

One final flaw in the city's position—a disadvantage that could not have been anticipated before the massive industrialization of the 20th Century began—is that the surrounding mountains trap the modern city's polluted air. As a result, Mexico City is now roofed by a more or less constant canopy of smog. Winds are rarely strong enough to carry the contaminated air over the mountain rim of the valley, and when the gusty winds called *nortes* (northers) do blow (usually between October and February) they are likely to aggravate the problem by sweeping over the city tons of yellow detritus from the dried-up bed of Lake Texcoco on the north-eastern outskirts. Moreover, at this high altitude there is 23 per cent less oxygen in the air than occurs at sea-level; consequently petrol burnt in such atmospheric conditions produces more than the normal amount of carbon monoxide, while the strong ultraviolet light from the sun produces an exaggerated photochemical effect on hydrocarbons in the air, so increasing the quantities of secondary pollutants, including eye-smarting nitrogenous compounds. It has been estimated that since 1937 daylight visibility has dropped from an average of 10 miles to about seven and a half miles.

Mexico City has succumbed, almost certainly irreversibly, to the condition known to Mexicans as *macrocefalia*—the sickness of top-heaviness. It is now so heavily industrialized that it accounts for approximately 60 per cent of the country's total manufacturing output. Concentrated unfor-

In this view to the north-west over Mexico City's business district, the great circle of the Plaza Insurgentes appears as a hub in the sprawling web of streets.

tunately in the north, so that prevailing winds carry industrial fumes back over the city, are cement works, an oil refinery, food processing plants, potteries and factories producing industrial chemicals, cars and all kinds of consumer goods. The combination of such industrial centralization with a rapid population growth and a massive citywards migration of workers has caused the city to grow to its present phenomenal size from a mere 1.5 million in 1940. Almost a fifth of Mexico's population is now crammed into less than a thousandth part of its territory.

The growth of rival cities, such as Monterrey in the north with its heavy industry, or the rapidly developing oil centres of Tampico on the Gulf Coast and of Villahermosa, has done little to reverse the process. In the 1970s, provincials seeking better job opportunities and landless peasants fleeing rural poverty were arriving in Mexico City at an estimated peak rate of almost a thousand a day. They had been warned by public posters in their villages and towns of the city's smog and overcrowding; still they came and here they still stay. The poorest of them are driven by the same necessity and lack of opportunity that sends many more hundreds of thousands illegally across the United States border in the north to work clandestinely at unskilled, underpaid labours. An estimated three-quarters of Mexico City's inhabitants live in inferior or slum dwellings, and more than a third of the work-force is underemployed or unemployed.

Although Mexico City qualifies as an environmental nightmare of the first magnitude, it is entirely possible to visit it and conclude that it is still one of the world's most beautiful capitals—a magnificent illusion that is most likely to be achieved if the visitor flies in by night, as I did on my first visit, and does not stray too far off the well-worn tourist track.

The first sight of the city, as you fly over the brim of the surrounding mountains to land almost a mile and a half above sea-level, is a truly breathtaking experience. The city's extraordinary growth across the Valley of Mexico has enhanced the spectacular night approach: one suddenly beholds a kaleidoscope of gleaming lights—not just whites but brilliant emeralds, yellows, reds, purples and blues—as though all the gems from a Spanish treasure chest had been spilt over the ground below.

Night-time illuminations also serve as a useful guide to the city's layout, especially when viewed in relative close-up from the 44-storey Latin American Tower, the tallest building in the city's central zone. Surpassed only by the Hotel de Mexico, which is eight floors higher and three and a half miles away to the south-west, the tower is strategically placed at a point where the old Spanish colonial city gives way to the most modern sector. From the tower's observatory one can see the main squares, avenues and streets picked out in lights like a diagram.

Six blocks away to the east, great chains of lights mark avenues converging on the heart of the capital: the Plaza de la Constitución, a vast

Settling beside a simple street display of nuts and tangerines in the Plaza de Santa Catarina, a woman offers her small child a fruit. Casual, small-scale vending is quite commonplace in a city that chronically suffers from massive unemployment and where many mothers struggle to raise children on uncertain incomes.

ceremonial square with sides more than 250 yards long. In the 14th and 15th Centuries, before the Spanish Conquest, this was the religious and political centre of the Aztec empire. Thereafter, during the 300 years of Spanish rule, the plaza served many purposes: a stage for extravagant pageants, a public execution ground, a fairground and a market. Here the New World had its first church, and in the immediate vicinity its first hospital and its first library. Here also, in August, 1529—only eight years after the Conquest—the first recorded bullfight in Mexico was staged. Bullfighting became so popular that on one occasion—to celebrate the arrival of a new archbishop from Spain—no fewer than a hundred bulls were fought and killed in three days.

The original church, built in 1525, has been replaced by the huge Metropolitan Cathedral that now stands on the north side of the plaza. On the east side is the monumental National Palace, housing the offices of the republic's government behind its 225-yard long, uniform façade. Twin municipal palaces, housing the administrative offices of the city, complete the south flank. The west side is distinguished by a severe, reddish-brick building that houses the National Pawnshop; founded in the 18th Century by a philanthropic nobleman, the pawnshop provides low-interest loans and is now run by the State.

The Plaza de la Constitución has been universally known as the Zócalo, meaning a base or plinth, ever since the mid-19th Century. One story goes that the plaza was so named when plans to adorn it with a monument to Mexico's independence from Spain, achieved in 1821, went no further than the laying of the memorial's foundation. Isolated and forlorn, the

TACUBA

Calzada General Mariano Escobedo

Avenida Marina Nacional

Calzada Mexico Tacuba

SANTA JULIA

Avenida Ribera de San Cosme

Avenida Thiers

Frontón Mexico

POLANCO

National Museum of
Anthropology

Avenida de los Insurgentes

Paseo de la Reforma

El Caba
Stat

Christopher
Columbus
Statue

Melchor Ocampo

Cuauhtemoc Statue

ZONA ROSA

JUAREZ

Chapultepec
Castle

Independence Monument

Plaza
Insurgentes

Casa del Lago
Cultural
Centre

Museum of
Modern Art

Zoo

Avenida Chapultepec

Chapultepec Park

Monument to the
Boy Heroes

Avenida Oaxaca

Avenida Álvaro Obregón

Avenida Cuauhtemoc

Periférico

Avenida Constituyentes

Avenida Tamaulipas

Dr. Pa

Church of Santiago
Tlatelolco

Plaza of the Three Cultures

TEPITO

● Thieves' Market
● Lagunilla Market

Plaza de
Santa Caterina

● Tenampa Saloon
Plaza
Garibaldi

Arena
● Coliseo

Church of
● Santo Domingo

Chamber of
● Deputies   Cathedral

Tacuba Street

Guatemala Street

Palace of   Central
Fine Arts   Post
               Office

Avenida
Juarez

Latin
American
Tower

Plaza de la
Constitución
(Zócalo)

City Hall ●   National Palace

National
● Library

Hospicio de
Jesús Nazareño ●

Merced Market

DOCTORES

Sonora
Market

Calzada Niño Perdido

José T. Cuellar

Calzada San Antonio Abad

Jamaica
Market

U.S.A.

MEXICO

Rio Grande

Monterrey ●

Gulf of Mexico

Tropic of Cancer

Teotihuacán   ● Tampico
Querétaro ●
Guadalajara ●   Mexico
Toluca ●   ● City
Cuernavaca ●   ● ● Veracruz   ● Villahermosa
Ixtaccihuatl 15,082 ft   BELIZE
Acapulco ●   Popocatepetl 17,520 ft   HONDURAS
Puebla   GUATEMALA

Pacific Ocean

The World's Largest City

Mexico City lies within the tropics, but at a cool altitude of 7,500 feet on the central Mexican plateau (inset map, above). Founded in the 14th Century by Aztec Indians on a lake-bounded island and rebuilt 200 years later by Spanish invaders, it has mushroomed during the 20th Century to become the largest city in the world, with an estimated population of more than 13 million.

Most of the city's historic landmarks are clustered in the original, central zone (main map). Around it sprawls the 289-square-mile modern conurbation, overflowing in many places the limits of the Federal District—the city's official administrative area (dotted line on inset map, below).

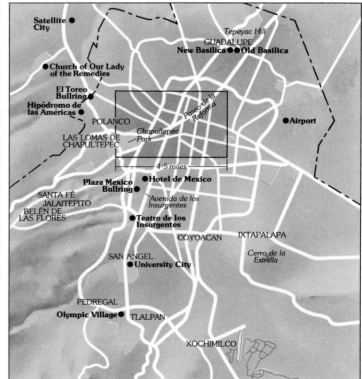

Satellite ●
City

Tepeyac Hill

GUADALUPE
New Basilica ●● Old Basilica

● Church of Our Lady
of the Remedies

● El Toreo
Bullring

Hipódromo de
las Américas ●

Paseo de la Reforma

POLANCO

Chapultepec
Park

● Airport

LAS LOMAS DE
CHAPULTEPEC

4-5 miles

Plaza Mexico ●   ● Hotel de Mexico
Bullring

SANTA FÉ
JALAITEPITO
BELÉN DE
LAS FLORES

Avenida de los
Insurgentes

● Teatro de los
Insurgentes

COYOACAN   IXTAPALAPA

Cerro de la
Estrella

SAN ANGEL
● University City

PEDREGAL

Olympic Village ●   ● TLALPAN

XOCHIMILCO

unfinished monument remained there for 77 years, its completion interrupted again and again by the political disturbances and foreign interventions that marked the first century of Mexico's development as an independent nation. Meanwhile the initially derisive expression "going to the *zócalo*" became established in the language, as a synonym for going to the plaza. Today every Mexican town has its *zócalo* or main square, featuring a church and town hall. But there is only one Zócalo; the heart of the Mexican nation.

Almost directly at the foot of the Latin American Tower on its northwest side, the greenery of the small and elegant Alameda Park glows with the soft phosphorescence of myriad lamps arranged in traditional Spanish clusters of five globes—a far cry from colonial times, when it was lit by the flames of religious fanaticism; for Alameda is the site of the Plaza del Quemadero (the Square of the Burning Place) where the "Holy Office" of the Spanish Inquisition ordered heretics and sorcerers to be burnt alive. (It allowed lesser offenders the privilege of being strangled beforehand.)

To the east side of Alameda, the streets follow the orderly layout of the Spanish colonial city; but to the west, the symmetrical grid gives way to a confused pattern of streets criss-crossing at every conceivable angle. Amid the confusion two enormous avenues, brightly lit, stand out: the Avenida de los Insurgentes and the Paseo de la Reforma. The former, usually referred to simply as Insurgentes, is named for those who rose against Spain in the Mexican War of Independence of 1810-21. The lights of the avenue, which is 14 miles long, stretch away seemingly without end to the north and to the south.

The Paseo de la Reforma (known as Reforma) is the capital's other main artery and the handsomest of all its streets. A great eight-lane boulevard, flanked by brightly lit skyscrapers and punctuated by illuminated monuments at many of its important intersections, it bisects the city's central zone from north-east to south-west. It crosses Insurgentes at a slant and disappears to the west into the darkness of Chapultepec Park, a thousand acres of public woodland where once the Aztec emperors had their private pleasure gardens, and now the President of the Republic has his official residence within a walled compound.

Reforma has a Parisian magnificence about it—and that is no accident. The avenue was laid in 1865 for the ill-fated Maximilian, an Austrian archduke who briefly and incongruously became Emperor of Mexico. In 1863, as the pawn of the opportunistic Napoleon III of France, Maximilian was enthroned by a French invasion force, and until his deposition and death in front of a Mexican firing-squad in 1867, he brought a French-supported splendour to Mexico City. The great boulevard was designed to allow the Emperor to drive in style from his castle residence in Chapultepec Park to the National Palace on the Zócalo. The name Reforma, however, given in 1870, commemorates the liberal laws enacted by Benito Juarez, the

Boys lounge outside a row of multi-hued homes.

White dresses stand out against a coral wall.

A Flair for Colour

On a multitude of building façades in the poorer residential districts of the city, the people's natural sense of colour expresses itself with tropical vibrancy. The simple frontages of *vecindades* (tenement homes) and *pulquerías* (bars selling a cheap alcoholic drink called *pulque*) have been transformed by coats of brilliant greens, blues, reds and yellows into striking visions of abstract street art. In Aztec times, colours held symbolic meaning—green for royalty, blue for sacrifice, yellow for food. No such formal code exists today, but glowing tones everywhere testify to the instinct towards vivid hues.

Green doors belong to a bar reserved for women.

More sober colours decorate a local pulqueria.

A red door blazes in a turquoise and blue wall.

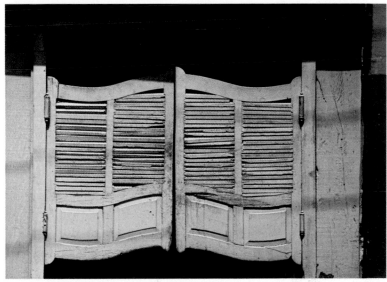

Light blue paint freshens up battered swing-doors.

Yellow and red walls combine for a cheery effect.

A youth helps to renew the city's coat of colour.

man who ordered Maximilian's execution, and was the first full-blooded Indian to be elected to the presidency. (The post was previously held by men of Spanish or mestizo blood.)

By day the same panoramic view of Mexico City from the Latin American Tower observatory expands, but it acquires the greyer tones of everyday reality. In the centre you can see ultra-modern structures crowding in on colonial and 19th-Century buildings. To the west, beyond Chapultepec Park, lie exclusive residential districts in the switchback region known as Las Lomas (The Hills). Away to the south there are a few other fashionable districts; notably San Angel—a charming, unspoilt, colonial suburb; Coyoacan, where the Spanish conquistador Hernán Cortés built his palace and where in 1940 Leon Trotsky was assassinated in his last retreat; and Pedregal, where some of the city's most modernistic homes are landscaped into a rocky terrain of black lava.

In every other direction, the muddled core of the city is surrounded by a characterless jumble of buildings stretching away over the valley as far as the eye can see. Groups of high-rise condominium apartments here and there punctuate the sea of two- or three-storey, concrete, low-cost housing estates, single-storey adobe dwellings and huddled *jacales*— shacks or shanties constructed of wood, cardboard and flattened jerry-cans. Slums and squatter settlements—sometimes called *ciudades perdidas* (lost cities)—are scattered through the urban sprawl and fill vacant land on the outskirts. Until a few decades ago this view was at least given some dignity by a dramatic backdrop to the south-east: the distant snow-capped peaks of two volcanic mountains, Popocatepetl and Ixtac-cihuatl (pronounced PopocaTEYpetl and IshtaSEEwatl); but those legendary peaks are now rarely seen through the polluted haze.

Down in the streets the pace and hubbub of the living city instantly takes hold. I remember vividly the first time I strolled down Reforma. Like Main Street in any 20th-Century metropolis, it was a multi-decibel hive of activity and commerce, teeming with pedestrians and traffic, clamorous with horn blasts, screeching brakes and the shrill notes of police whistles. Everywhere there was something to divert the eye: a baker's boy bicycling by with a bread basket miraculously balanced on his head; a young man serving hot coffee from a huge container strapped on his back; street vendors peddling wares to motorists at every traffic-light; legions of shoe-shine boys and lottery-ticket sellers touting for custom; a man entertaining passers-by with his dancing bear; a fire-eater breathing out flames; a truck daubed with the message "Pass me . . . your wife"; traffic cops stylishly dressed in light blue uniforms (with white turtle-neck sweaters) and wearing their ·38 specials strapped low in open holsters, ready for a quick draw exactly like gunfighters in a Western.

Indian women offered straw goods for sale, or textiles—especially *sarapes*, the striped woollen cloaks traditionally worn by Mexican men. A

Near Alameda Park, twin buildings belonging to the Department of the Navy lean away from each other as a result of uneven subsidence of their foundations. Much of Mexico City stands on land reclaimed since the 17th Century from lakes, and the subsoil is still spongy. Some of the old buildings have sunk as much as several feet within the past half century alone.

few women were unobtrusively begging, usually with at least one small, pathetic-looking child in tow, or else a baby hidden inside a *rebozo*, the all-purpose cotton shawl that is cradle, handbag and shopping basket combined. These women are colloquially known as "Marías", a term of obscure origin. A popular explanation is that, in the past, when Spanish priests were converting the rural Indian population to Christianity, they routinely baptized women with the name María, and it came to be applied to all rural women—mostly Indian—who moved into the city to beg. The children accompanying them, I discovered, are not always the beggars' own; the youngsters may be hired through a middle man for the day to soften the hearts of solvent shoppers.

At the junction of Reforma and Insurgentes, I turned south-west into the Zona Rosa, or Pink Zone, a cosmopolitan enclave of about one square mile that includes gourmet restaurants, sidewalk cafés and elegant boutiques. The origin of its name is uncertain, but it fits. This is the city's most fashionable shopping quarter, both for tourists and wealthier citizens. It is especially renowned for the excellence of its restaurants, which serve not only Mexico's own distinctive cooking (such as *mole poblano*—a famous dish of turkey in a sauce made with chili, chocolate and sesame seeds—and dozens of dishes based on the traditional chilies and beans) but also a high standard of most other national cuisines.

In a charming pedestrian side-street lined with miniature trees and potted plants I sat outside a restaurant—mock Tudor in style, as it happened—waiting for a lunch appointment I had with an American long-term resident. Nearby, an accordionist who was thumbing out a merry tune competed with an *organillero* cranking a portable organ. When the American arrived, he immediately began to lament that I could not have seen Mexico City as it was in the 1950s, when the traffic was still bearable and the air fit to breathe. "Isn't it awful?" he asked rhetorically. "The traffic is getting worse every day. And the pollution is already impossible. Do you know that a scientist recently put three cages of rabbits on the sidewalk in front of the Latin American Tower and within three hours all the rabbits had died of asphyxiation?"

I had, of course, already observed that the city's buses invariably billowed black trails of diesel smoke, and thought it fortunate that some, at least, were fitted with overhead exhausts so that noxious fumes did not hit pedestrians directly in the face. Nonetheless, I could honestly tell my American friend that I barely noticed the pollution at the time; although the overall image of the city constantly appeared hazy, the foreground remained strongly in focus and insistently bombarded the senses. The most striking impression was the profusion of colour: the red and yellow banks of freshly cut flowers for sale; the vivid hues of clothing, both men's and women's; the lavish displays of produce in the open-air markets; and the brilliantly coloured mosaics that decorated a number of the newer buildings.

Elegant flights of stairs connect the three floors of the opulent Central Post Office on Tacuba Street. The building, designed in 1904 by the Italian architect Adamo Boari, is one of the city's most notable examples of the ornate style popular at the turn of the century.

The prevalence of vast murals in Mexico City owes much to the upsurge of nationalism that followed the Mexican Revolution of 1910-20. This savage upheaval, which aimed at redistributing land from the great estates of the 19th Century, and for the first time brought the mestizo and Indian masses into the body politic, was boldly commemorated by post-revolutionary governments from the 1920s onwards. They commissioned numerous artists to adorn the interiors of public buildings and schools with murals glorifying the country's Indian tradition, the revolutionary struggle of the peasants and the ideals of the new order. Among the most gifted and prolific of the artists to emerge were three whose names have become known world-wide: Diego Rivera, José Clemente Orozco and David Alfaro Siqueiros.

Later governments commissioned artists to decorate exterior walls. The University of Mexico City—the first such institution in the Americas, founded in 1551—has an ultra-modern campus begun in 1950, with a library entirely clothed in mosaic designs by the painter-architect Juan O'Gorman. The façade of the Teatro de los Insurgentes flames with a colourful mosaic frieze by Diego Rivera, completed in 1953.

Complementing the array of primary colours is the climate, one of the city's unique gifts. Though Mexico City is on the same latitude as such torrid and oppressive spots as Bombay and Haiti, the altitude ensures that it is rarely uncomfortably hot, humid or cold. The city enjoys a year-round mean temperature of about 65°F, with a seasonal variation between "winter" and "summer" of a mere 5°F. On most days of the year the weather forecast is predictably "sunny and warm", and reliable enough for the city's Hipódromo de las Américas to stage a horse-racing season of 11 months, claimed as the longest in the world.

Seasons in the Valley of Mexico can be divided fairly precisely into the dry months (October to April) and the rainy months (May to September). In the rainy season, black storm clouds may gather suddenly and release a torrential downpour, accompanied by a sudden plunge in temperature. Just as suddenly, the clouds disappear and the city's rainbow of colours glistens anew in the sunlight. Wintry weather barely exists; a mild snowfall is such a novelty—occurring perhaps once or twice in a generation—that it is greeted by both young and old with near hysterical excitement.

I have only once witnessed a Mexican snowfall and the scenes were unforgettable, as though all of Mexico City had been gripped by gold-rush fever. During the three-day cold snap, hundreds of thousands of citizens drove to the outlying hills to enjoy the pristine white blanket of snow, mostly no more than an inch or two thick, before it disappeared. When I myself went up on the second day, I found scenes of near pandemonium. People were cramming the snow excitedly into plastic bags, hoping to get it home and hoard it along with their frozen foods. I actually heard growlings among late-comers about early diggers who had taken more than their share. Even if it meant shaking snow from trees and scraping it from rocky slopes, almost every family constructed a snowman and perched it on top of their car to take back into town. During the long crawl home, some young men rode perilously on the car roofs to hold their snowmen steady. Once down from the high ground swept by frigid winds, the snowmen began to shrink; but the freakish temperature was still low enough—only a few degrees above freezing—for many of them to survive the journey. Some even lasted a few hours after arrival, much to the delight of their enthusiastic creators.

The evenings, too, are normally mild and so the city's outdoor life goes on late. I remember exploring after dark one evening north of the Zócalo, beyond the ornate bulk of the Metropolitan Cathedral, and finding myself in an extraordinary open-air office. It was the Plaza Santo Domingo, once known as "The Square of the Scribes". One colonnaded side of the square was occupied by Mexicans pecking at typewriters and operating antique printing-presses. Here, as in colonial times, professional scribes worked beneath dimly lit arches to serve the illiterate. As with the quill-pen-pushers of old, a typist could still be paid a few pesos to help compose a stylish love letter—although usually, as I saw, the work was rather less inviting. Most of the scribes were busy typing official correspondence, filling in tax declarations, printing personal business cards and generally feeding the Mexican bureaucracy with the official forms it demands in triplicate or more.

Two blocks west of Santo Domingo, high-pitched trumpet sounds lured me into a square of an entirely different kind: the Plaza Garibaldi, traditional gathering-place of the city's renowned street musicians, the *mariachis*. I had been told that this was the vigorous hub of an area of bawdy *cantinas* (bars), and dark goings-on. But I had arrived about 10 p.m.—long before there was any sign on its cobbled streets of the excesses wrought by tequila, the fiery Mexican spirit distilled from the juice of the agave cactus. The atmosphere at that hour was totally seductive.

Mexico City has several distinct types of street musician, including guitar trios and Veracruzian groups with guitars and harp; but the most numerous are the *mariachis*, traditionally clad in black suits derived from formal dress of the 18th Century. All over the square customers were clustered around groups of *mariachis*—each including guitarists, violinists and trumpeters—who for a standard fee performed romantic or stirring ballads. Music and song from more than a hundred different musicians filled the air. Surprisingly, even with all the bands playing in one area, there was none of the expected cacophony, since the square was large enough to allow the music to disperse. Only the penetrating tones of the trumpets soared clear above the pleasurable musical hubbub. In the relaxed and joyful atmosphere, even the policemen standing about beside the square's illuminated fountain were paying to have songs played.

More recently, I have become familiar enough with the Plaza Garibaldi to be well aware of its seedy side: the prostitution, the drunkenness and

In Jamaica Market, a flower and vegetable trading centre near the heart of the capital, a consignment of crimson blooms is sold off piecemeal to an eager throng of flower vendors who operate stalls elsewhere in the capital. A love of flowers has always been characteristic of Mexicans: the ancient Aztecs named one of the months of their calendar Tlaxochimaco, meaning "the birth of the flowers".

On the roof of a house in the modern suburb of Satellite City, eight miles from the centre of the capital, the smooth lines of two brightly painted water tanks and their white supporting cradles reflect the artistic flair that Mexicans bring even to functional objects.

squalor that invade the adjacent back-streets in the small hours. But I must confess that it did entrance me completely at first sight. I loved its vigorous ambience and its haunting sounds, and I especially warmed to the famous Tenampa Saloon, the largest of several bars on the square, and one with a secure place in the folklore of the city. It was opened as a small bar in the 1920s and soon became a favourite meeting-place for the *mariachis*. In the 1940s it achieved considerable notoriety for its scenes of riotous disorder. Nowadays, greatly enlarged and much more respectable, it is on the tourist circuit. Three and a half million people visit Mexico every year and a fair number end up "slumming", as more than one guidebook puts it, in the Plaza Garibaldi. During the peak season from December to January, the Tenampa is sometimes crowded with foreigners, and boasts that it has been patronized by a host of notable visitors, ranging from Elizabeth Taylor to the late Emperor Haile Selassie of Ethiopia.

Maybe it is artfully contrived for the tourists—the wooden swing-doors leading directly on to the long bar, where almost every customer seems to be drinking straight tequila, with the obligatory salt and lime, and a tomato-juice chaser. But it is the only bar in town that faintly evokes my movie-shaped images of a rowdy Mexican *cantina*, and it is a good place to observe Mexican night-life.

My first visit to the bar was in late February. There were no tourists in sight and only two women that I could see, tucked away with their boy-friends in a corner cubicle. A small *mariachi* group—two violinists and a trumpeter—were playing for the couples in the corner. As the only non-Mexican, I was immediately made to feel welcome by an invitation to join a small group for a drink. As rounds of tequilas followed at a positively challenging rate, I became aware that, in this riotously convivial all-male environment, honour was everywhere at stake. In behaviour and conversation, the customers were playing the half-jocular, half-serious game of *machismo*—that very Mexican rivalry which casts every self-respecting male in the role of a matador on trial: ever ready to face his moment of truth, to prove his virility, to fulfil his masculine ego.

In one side-booth, opposite the long bar, two young men were locked grimly in an arm-wrestling hold. In another, a group of middle-aged men were noisily trying to prove their powers of resistance by taking it in turns to grip the copper leads from a multicoloured electric box. "Five pesos a shock," explained the owner of the box, Señor Cristino Anaya. "See how much you can take."

And when someone accepted the challenge, he steadily increased the voltage until the victim was compelled to let go. Two hundred volts was the maximum power of his box; Señor Anaya told me that the average breaking-point was around 80. Only one man, a crayon-portrait artist by the name of Martínez, who sold his sketches in the bar, had ever taken the full 200. Señor Anaya had been shocking people for eight years, he said. "I used to shine shoes but business was bad. So I converted my shoeshine box to electricity, and now I can earn twice as much."

Where else, I wondered, but among people with an incorrigibly competitive streak could a man earn a living by such a trade?

Most great cities are in some way confusing to the newcomer; but very few, I think, can be quite so confusing as Mexico City. Some of my initial perplexities, of course, were just the superficial misunderstandings of the new arrival. I had been in the city several days on my first visit before I realized that when people referred to "Mexico", they were not talking, as I thought, about the country, but about Mexico City and the Federal District that administers the capital. The country as a whole—consisting of 31 states plus the Federal District—is usually referred to as *la república*. To add to my confusion, there is a state of Mexico adjoining the Federal District, with its own capital of Toluca.

Another temporary misunderstanding led me, foolishly, to wait in my apartment for a Mexican friend who had told me, "I will see you tomorrow at your house." He never showed up. I should have worked it out: when a Mexican says *"su casa"* (your house) he really means "my house"—a common courtesy indicating that you are so welcome that his home is yours.

Again, in Mexico City the arrangement of house numbers at first seems to defy rational explanation. Streets change their name in mid-route so that you may find house Number 6 next to house Number 104. Of course! A Mexican will tell you it is perfectly logical. The change of name means the street has entered a different *colonia*, as the city's one thousand or so neighbourhoods are called. I gradually came to see that the arrangement even has its advantages, since every *colonia* uses a different class of street names. Thus, if you know someone lives on a street called Londres or

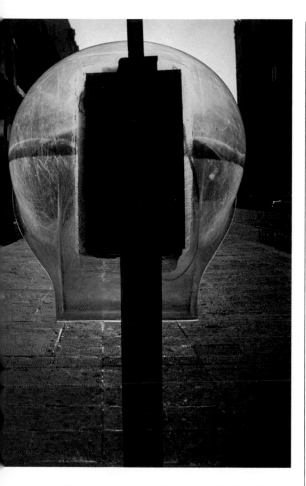

The morning sun illuminates the translucent, yellow plastic shield of a public telephone booth. Use of the sidewalk units is inexpensive and so they are in constant demand among the many who have no telephone at home. Most of Mexico City's subscribers are businesses and other commercial enterprises.

Liverpool or Hamburgo, you know automatically that they live in Colonia Juarez, the district where streets are named after European cities. Similarly anyone who lives in Colonia Doctores must live on a street with the name of a famous doctor, and so on.

Such initial puzzles are of course soon cleared up. Others are harder to reconcile. Indeed, it takes a measure of Orwellian doublethink to accommodate the many contradictions in Mexico's political and religious life.

Nine-tenths of Mexico's population profess Roman Catholicism, and the capital has 726 Catholic churches. Yet, this is a city where—on paper at least—it is against the law for the Church to own one square foot of land or one brick of property, and where anticlerical laws exist to forbid priests and nuns to wear their robes in the streets. Mexico is the only Latin American country to have no diplomatic relations with the Vatican; yet in 1979 the Pope made a six-day visit and was welcomed by the President.

In spite of its boulevards named Reforma and Insurgentes, and its public buildings ablaze with gigantic frescos extolling socialist ideals, the city is the centre of a straightforwardly capitalist economy. The constitution describes a democratic government on traditional liberal lines, but one party holds a monopoly of power. It goes by the thought-provoking name of the Party of the Institutional Revolution (Partido Revolucionario Institucional, or PRI for short) and is the direct heir of this century's Revolution; yet, its policies for the most part are conservative and its structure authoritarian, and it incorporates within it all significant political forces.

Still another contradictory aspect of the city is its relationship with the United States, the immense northern neighbour that Mexicans call *el coloso del norte* (the giant of the north). Mexico City is the Latin American capital closest to the United States, some 500 miles from the border. Its inhabitants are constantly emulating the riches and modernity of the States, and they are generally doing a pretty good job of turning their capital into an American city. At the same time, however, the city preserves a strong and touchy awareness that it is the frontier town of Latin Americanism. It is the capital of a Spanish-speaking, Catholic, developing nation confronting the English-speaking, Anglo-Saxon, Protestant, developed civilization of North America.

But given some knowledge of history, one finds sane reasons for such schizoid patterns. Today's restricted position of the Catholic Church, for example, makes some sense in the light of the excesses of colonial times, when the Church came to own more than half the land and buildings in Mexico. Reforms in the 19th Century were designed to break its much resented power, and the revolutionary constitution of 1917 reinforced the inflexible separation of Church and State, decreeing, for example, that priests may not play any part in politics or education. In theory, these rulings still stand, but they are not strictly enforced. A pragmatic co-operation between Church and State has replaced what were once very bitter hostilities indeed; and the bulk of the population, unmoved by political considerations, remains loyal to the Mexican style of Catholicism.

As an Englishman with a conventional view of the British-pattern parliamentary democracy, I shall probably always see some contrariety in Mexico's form of government. The President is elected by direct universal suffrage, and that seems democratic enough. But there is never any doubt about the outcome of an election, since the candidate of the omnipotent PRI is always successful. As the representative of the governing party he has nation-wide publicity and a campaign management that the small opposition parties cannot hope to match. The real choice is made within the party, not by the electorate. Once in office the President has a six-year term, during which his power is virtually unlimited; he appoints many officials directly—including the *jefe* of the Federal District, the administrative head of Mexico City. He has total control of foreign relations and an absolute veto over laws passed by the elective Congress. The only significant formal check on his power is that he can never be re-elected.

Yet, whatever the system's peculiarity, the defence of Mexico's form of democracy is that it works. Mexico has enjoyed more than half a century of economic and social progress under the same constitution, and administrations have succeeded one another peacefully ever since the formation of the party in 1929—no mean achievement when compared with the record of fellow Latin American states.

The biggest puzzle of all in Mexico City is the people. Frenetic and competitive one moment, leisurely, Latin and engaging the next, they present a constant riddle to the spectator. Mexicans, it seems, accept contradictions as part of life, and feel little need to try to resolve them. The same mestizo taxi-driver may, to one passenger, claim Hispanic descent and express contempt for the Indian, and to the next—with equal sincerity and pride— declare absolute solidarity with the Aztec past. The soft-spoken circuitous courtesy of so many Mexicans makes them the soul of consideration; but beneath it one senses a daunting reserve, and sometimes a latent violence. Mexicans are usually fiercely nationalistic, yet they can display a jeering scepticism, on occasions such as a President's inaugural address on radio or television, that makes them appear wholly subversive.

Growing acquaintance with Mexico City confirmed rather than dispelled my puzzlement, and I concluded that I had hit on something fundamental. I found that others had felt the same. Octavio Paz, probably Mexico's best known modern poet and a penetrating analyst of the nature of his fellow Mexicans, writes in his book *The Labyrinth of Solitude*: "The details of the image formed of us often vary with the spectator, but it is always an ambiguous, if not a contradictory image. . . . Treachery, loyalty, crime and love hide out in the depths of our glance. . . . We are enigmatic not only to strangers, but also to ourselves. The Mexican is always a problem, both for other Mexicans and for himself."

Vistas of the Night

At dusk the summit of the 17,520-foot-high volcano Popocatepetl, 40 miles south-east of the city centre, glows above the scattered lights of outlying districts.

In Mexico City dusk comes early—at about 6 p.m. in winter and only an hour or so later in summer. As the daylight rapidly fades, the ungainly sprawl of the city's outlying colonies and industrial zones is registered in the countless pinpricks of light that spread across the high Valley of Mexico. Avenues such as the great Paseo de la Reforma—laid out during the brief reign of the Emperor Maximilian in the 1860s—rule their straight lines across the city, recalling the time when the capital began to acquire a new European splendour. Floodlights give back to selected landmarks the prominence their planners intended; the rays pick out the grandiose public buildings with which the dictator Porfirio Díaz adorned the city in the early 20th Century, and bring into focus some of the bold, rectilinear developments created since the 1950s by Mexico's pioneering architects.

Rush-hour traffic inches along the Paseo de la Reforma, past islanded statues. The column (top, centre) is the Independence Monument.

Painted concrete pillars up to 170 feet high, designed by sculptor Matías Goeritz, mark the approaches to modern, suburban Satellite City.

At the east end of Alameda Park, strategically placed floodlights bathe the Palace of Fine Arts, designed for President Díaz in 1904 but not finished until 19

ice then, the massive, marbled building—which houses art galleries, exhibition rooms and concert halls—has sunk eight feet into the city's soft subsoil.

24
DE
DICIEMBRE
FELIZ
100
MILLONES
DE PESOS
DICIEMBRE 16
DIA DEL BILLETERO
merican
Airlines

Festooned in neon, the National Lottery Building stands 18 storeys high at the corner of Reforma and Avenida Juarez outshining the floodlit equestrian statue of a Spanish king, Charles IV (foreground). Profits from the lottery help to finance welfare facilities such as orphanages and hospitals for the city.

Competing with the glare from two light-filled avenues—Juarez (centre) and Hidalgo (right)—forked lightning crackles above the city's western outskirts.

2

The Aztec Heritage

In November 1519, Cortés and his force of Spanish soldiers became the first Europeans to lay eyes on the city of Mexico-Tenochtitlan, capital of the Aztec empire. Reporting to King Charles I of Spain, in whose name he had made the 250-mile march from the coast into the heart of Aztec territory, Cortés wrote that it was "the most beautiful city in the world". Years later, a hard-bitten fellow soldier, Bernal Díaz del Castillo, tried and failed to do justice to the feelings of the Spaniards on that occasion: "We were amazed," he wrote in his invaluable first-hand record, *The True History of the Conquest of New Spain*, "and said it was like the enchantments they tell of in the legend of Amadis, on account of the great towers and *cués* [temples] and buildings rising from the water, and all built of masonry. And some of our soldiers even asked whether the things that we saw were not a dream? It is not to be wondered at that I here write it down in this manner, for there is so much to think over that I do not know how to describe it, seeing things as we did that had never been heard of or seen before, not even dreamed about."

The city that they saw spread before them was indeed a wonder of the world. Its population equalled or exceeded that of any city in Europe at the time, and its layout was bewitching. An island-metropolis, Tenochtitlan was set like a radiant jewel amid the clear, calm turquoise of saline Lake Texcoco, linked to mainland suburbs by three great paved causeways. Elegant palaces and pyramidal temples, interspersed with broad plazas and exotic gardens, gleamed spotless white in the brilliant crystalline air more than 7,000 feet above sea-level.

Most extraordinary of all, this gigantic city—centre of an empire that held sway over 5 or 6 million people—had been no more than a cluster of reed huts only two centuries before. By the time the Aztecs set about building their capital, a whole series of civilizations had waxed and waned in middle America. The Mayan sites of the tropical Yucatan, dating to the 4th Century A.D., and the huge complex of ancient buildings to be seen at Teotihuacan, 30 miles north-east of Mexico City, still testify to the scale of Indian accomplishment during the first millennium. But after the decline of these cultures, from A.D. 900 onwards, warlike peoples from the north intruded into middle America. Among the last arrivals, according to their own traditions, were the Mexica, one of several Nahuatl-speaking tribes now loosely described as Aztec.

When the Mexica first appeared in the 12th Century, they may have been no more than a thousand strong, an insignificant force of squatters

The staring eyes and ghastly grimace of a skull-like religious image in the National Museum of Anthropology evoke the grim preoccupation with death that haunted the Aztecs, the Indian nation whose capital, Tenochtitlan, became Mexico City. The statue represents one of the malevolent demons known as Cihuateteo: women who, after death in childbirth, returned to earth to inflict evil on the living.

attempting to make their home among the well-established states in the Basin of Mexico. For a while, the Mexica existed on the sufferance of cities that could use them as mercenaries in their frequent wars. But in the 14th Century (Aztec annals give a probable date of 1325), they founded their own city of Mexico-Tenochtitlan on a small rocky island among the reeds and swampy marshes of Lake Texcoco. According to legend, they chose the site because of a prophecy that they were to prosper where they saw an eagle devouring a snake while perched on a cactus growing on a stone —and such an eagle appeared to them on a rock in the lake. (Today the bird appears, with snake and cactus, as a stylized emblem on the Mexican flag.) Anyone dissatisfied with this explanation of Mexico City's position can assume that the land was available because the site was so unpromising.

Yet the Aztecs of Tenochtitlan flourished on the unwanted spot. The island had immense strategic value, both for military defence and as a trading centre for the many independent settlements dotted around the lake. Within a century of the founding of the city, the settlers were able to throw off the subject status they had previously been forced to accept, and embark on a career of conquest that brought them control of the enormous empire that was penetrated by the Spaniards in 1519.

The society of the Aztecs was complex, orderly and austere. The ruler of Tenochtitlan, who had absolute political, religious and military power, was chosen from among the male relatives of the previous ruler for his ability and rectitude, and was deeply venerated by all his subjects. Although social ranks were clearly defined, a certain degree of mobility was possible: within the ruling class, rank was attributed according to the office held, not by hereditary right; and it was possible for commoners to gain entry into the ruling class if they distinguished themselves in war.

One of the most remarkable characteristics of Aztec society was the place it gave to warfare. War was a recognized and even welcome institution, not a disaster; and all males from the age of 15 upwards had the obligation to bear arms whenever war was declared on another state. The main body of warriors was supplied by the commoners, led by a knightly élite under the supreme command of the emperor. Clad in quilted cotton armour, armies numbering many thousands launched themselves at each other with razor-sharp, obsidian-edged weapons. Conquest naturally yielded material and political advantages, since the defeated state was reduced to tribute-paying vassalage. But these were not the only motives for Aztec imperialist aggression: war was also intimately connected with religion.

The Aztec world believed in a complex pantheon of gods, compiled— not without some inconsistencies—by assimilating pre-Aztec beliefs to the worship of their own gods. The most prominent of the gods were Quetzalcoatl, the "Feathered Serpent", creator of mankind, who ruled the winds and had been worshipped by valley folk since long before the appearance of the Aztecs; Tlaloc, god of the rain, also very ancient; and

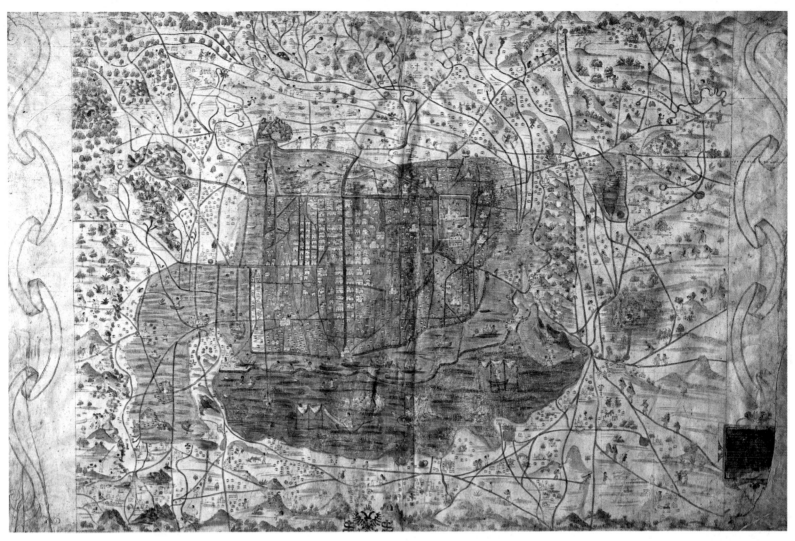

This mid-16th-Century landscape-map, painted on parchment and orientated with the west at the top, records Mexico City (brown area, centre) as it was only some 30 years after the Spanish Conquest in 1521. At that date, the surrounding lakes (blue-green area), with their teeming canoe traffic and maze of connecting causeways and canals remained substantially as they had been in Aztec times.

Tezcatlipoca, "Smoking Mirror", god of the night sky and protector of young warriors—a pre-Aztec deity with whom the Aztecs at least partially identified their own patron war god, Huitzilopochtli.

It was thought that Quetzalcoatl and the fierce Tezcatlipoca were locked in an eternal struggle that threatened the extinction of the world. The struggle had already caused the destruction and re-creation of the world four times, according to Aztec belief; and the warrior people considered it their special mission to try to preserve the fifth world in which they lived. This world might be prolonged only if the many gods were amply nourished with human blood offered to them, with due honour, by ritual sacrifice in their own temples. War, therefore, in which prisoners were taken to provide a constant supply of sacrificial victims, was a sacred duty to all devout Aztecs.

Many myths surrounded the all-important figure of Quetzalcoatl—and one of them was to be fateful. The Aztecs believed that, at some legendary period, this god of healing and learning, who alone deplored human sacrifice, had appeared on earth in human form—he had a white skin and a black beard—to bring civilizing knowledge to his followers. But Tezcatlipoca had worsted him in their continual struggle, and Quetzalcoatl had been driven away to the east. On leaving to reside in some mysterious land beyond the sea, he had despatched four of his attendants with the message, "I will return in a One Reed year to re-establish my rule."

In the complex Aztec calendar, successive years were designated by combining a name—Reed, Wind, House and so on—with a number. "One

Eagles of Good Omen

A snake-devouring eagle, incorporated since 1821 in the Mexican national insigne, appears everywhere in Mexico City: on buildings, flags and coinage; in murals, sculptures and stained-glass windows. Although savage in aspect, the eagle symbolizes prosperity, not aggression. According to ancient tradition, the site of the Aztec capital on a rocky island in Lake Texcoco was chosen in fulfilment of a prophecy that its founders would thrive where they saw an eagle settle to eat a snake on a cactus sprouting from a rock. (The words for "rock" and "cactus" in the Aztecs' Nahuatl language—*tetl* and *nochtli*—also yielded the name Tenochtitlan.)

The emblematic image of the eagle—with snake, cactus and stone—has been given a wide variety of artistic treatments. They range from the proud bird perched above the Central Post Office (top row, left) to the motif, in grimly Aztec style, above the entrance to the National Museum of Anthropology (top row, second from right). In Chapultepec Castle Museum, the eagle is emblazoned on the 19th-Century state coach of the Emperor Maximilian (centre row, second from left); and, scorning partiality, it adorns the brass bedstead of Maximilian's arch-enemy, Benito Juarez (centre row, second from right) in the same museum.

Reed" years fell at regular intervals, 52 years apart. The people of Mexico had repeatedly lived through One Reed years. Quetzalcoatl had not come.

In 1502, the Aztecs elected a new priest-king. Moctezuma II was a slender, thinly bearded man, deeply devout and learned, possessed of an exquisite refinement of both movement and manners. (The traditional spelling, "Montezuma", is the result of the Spaniards' first attempts to transcribe the unfamiliar sounds of Nahuatl; linguists now accept that "Moctezuma" is closer to the original.) At his accession Moctezuma heard astrologers prophesy that the world would end during his reign. Over the following years, his fears steadily mounted as he brooded over a growing number of portents of doom: comets streaking across the skies, electric storms, the Great Teocalli (temple) in Tenochtitlan mysteriously catching fire. Above all he was alarmed by reports, brought from the eastern reaches of the Aztec empire by the messengers of his efficient intelligence service—stories of men who rode on the sea in floating castles, who carried sticks that spat deadly fire, who crossed the land on armoured, hornless stags that snorted and bellowed and brought thunder from the earth beneath.

The next One Reed year was 1519. And on February 10, 1519, a Spanish expedition—11 ships carrying 508 swordsmen, 32 crossbowmen, 13 musketeers, 16 horses and 14 cannon—set sail from Havana in Cuba to explore the Mexican mainland, which had been discovered two years before by Spaniards who had landed in Mayan territory. In command was Hernán Cortés—white-skinned, black-bearded, and determined to conquer Mexico.

Son of a country squire of Extremadura in Spain, Cortés was born into an age designed for enterprise on the grand scale. In 1492, after almost 800 years of continual conflict, the Spaniards had finally cleared the Iberian peninsula of the last Moorish invaders. That same year, by his discovery of the West Indies, Columbus had provided a new outlet for the crusading spirit of a nation so long geared to fighting passionately in the name of God and country. Cortés, thirsting for adventure like thousands of young Spaniards before him, saw in the New World his hope of fame and fortune.

By 1518, Cortés was well established as a leading landowner on the island of Cuba. Excited by reports—gathered from Indians by Spanish exploratory expeditions to the mainland coast—telling of a gold-rich inland country called Mexico, he mortgaged his estates and, with other investors, sank all the proceeds into financing a major expedition. Diego Velázquez, Governor of Cuba, officially approved the enterprise in the name of Spain, but later he became so alarmed at the scale of the expedition that he withdrew his endorsement. It was too late. Cortés had already sailed. In open defiance of the Governor, Cortés headed west to Mexico.

Luck favoured him to an unusual degree. Indeed, good fortune blessed him from the moment he first approached the mainland and anchored at the island of Cozumel on the east coast of Yucatan. There he found a

The Pyramid of the Sun

The Temple of Quetzalcoatl

The Pyramid of the Moon

Teotihuacan, a ruined ceremonial city of pre-Aztec origin, is situated 30 miles north-east of the capital. Dominated by the 203-foot-high Pyramid of the Sun (top) and the 183-foot-high Pyramid of the Moon (bottom), the site covers eight square miles and embraces a complex of religious buildings, including the richly carved Temple of Quetzalcoatl, the serpent god (centre). On discovering this already deserted city in the 12th Century, the Aztecs were so awed by it that they named it Teotihuacan —the Place where One Becomes a God—and modelled their own temples on its architecture.

Spaniard named Aguilar who had been shipwrecked eight years earlier and had lived with the natives ever since. Aguilar spoke the Maya language and so from the start Cortés had a reliable interpreter.

Unfortunately, Aguilar did not speak Nahuatl, the tongue of the Mexicans whom the Spaniards would encounter when they explored further west. Again, Cortés was lucky. After winning his first major battle at Tabasco, the frontier region of Maya territory, the local lords brought him peace-offerings, including a gift of 20 women. Among these Indian women was one who spoke both Nahuatl and Maya. With her aid, and that of Aguilar, Cortés could now communicate with the emissaries of Moctezuma and, no less importantly, with tribes living under Mexican domination.

This woman, known to the Indians as Malinche, was to become so closely identified with Cortés that eventually he too was known to them as Malinche. Baptized Marina by a Spanish priest (since no conquistador was permitted to cohabit with a heathen), she was the first Mexican to become a Christian, and subsequently she served Cortés as interpreter, adviser, confidante and mistress. Her linguistic ability and political perception were so invaluable that, arguably, without her, Cortés might have failed to conquer Mexico. As a result, she is now the most denigrated woman in Mexican history. The name Malinche is comparable to that of Quisling in Europe, and *malinchista* is part of the modern Mexican language: derogatory slang for anyone who consorts with foreigners or shows preference for things foreign. It is a harsh epitaph for a brave and brilliant woman, more betrayed than betraying: although high-born, she had been given into slavery as a child by her own mother and had passed from tribe to tribe until she found status and self-respect with the invaders.

With the aid of Malinche, Cortés was able to exploit political weaknesses in an Aztec empire dominated, rather than governed, by the imperialistic might of Tenochtitlan. The Spaniards met Indians who cautiously welcomed them as challengers to the power of Moctezuma. More significantly, they came across one fiercely independent tribe (the Tlaxcalans) that was still defying the Aztecs after a hundred years of war. In September, the Tlaxcalans lost a hard-fought battle against the conquistadors, and then offered their support to the Spaniards—an alliance later to prove decisive in the final invasion of Tenochtitlan. A force of 6,000 friendly Indians joined the Spaniards on their march inland.

In many ways, of course, Cortés made his own luck by way of brilliant diplomacy mixed with sudden, unexpected acts of ruthless aggression. But his greatest luck was thrust upon him: the ever-present shadow of Quetzalcoatl. Matching as he did the god's description, appearing from the quarter where Quetzalcoatl had vanished, and in the predicted year, Cortés aroused from the start the fear that he might be the Feathered Serpent returning at last and that resistance was therefore doomed. So long as the true identity of Cortés remained in doubt, the brooding, omen-

racked Moctezuma hesitated to oppose him. Moctezuma sent out a succession of emissaries bearing gifts of gold and jewels, and offered to give Cortés an annual tribute of treasure, slaves or whatever else he wanted if only he would not enter the city. Hedging his bets on Cortés' godhood, Moctezuma tried having the Spaniards ambushed, but unsuccessfully. Cortés marched relentlessly on, a figure so commanding, so uncompromising, that belief in his divinity was steadily reinforced. When he finally approached the city, Moctezuma did not dare refuse him entry. Trusting to their God and sustained by their sense of historical mission, compelled by the all-or-nothing tactical necessity of controlling the nerve-centre of the Aztec empire, the Spaniards—a few hundred men surrounded by an enemy potentially at least a million strong—took the almost unbelievable risk of entering the island-city, where they must have known they could be extinguished at a moment's notice.

Moctezuma, still half convinced that he was dealing with gods, received them with honour and lodged them in a palace near his own. When the Spaniards demanded that he change his own lodging and join them,

This Aztec illustration—part of a manuscript drawn up for the Spaniards after the Conquest—records the empire-building feats of Axayacatl, a 15th-Century ruler of Tenochtitlan. The Aztecs had no alphabet but employed a precise if abbreviated picture-writing system to chronicle their history. The enthroned Axayacatl (far left) looks down on a row of emblems denoting nine towns he conquered. On the steps of a temple lie the dismembered remains of a defeated enemy, sacrificed according to Aztec custom and belief in order to propitiate the gods.

Moctezuma acquiesced in becoming their hostage. A strange six-month period ensued, during which the Spaniards lived in comfort, moving unmolested around the city, marvelling at its immensity and orderly bustle.

Tenochtitlan had long ago spilt over from the small island where it had been founded two centuries before. It had grown into a vast conurbation with thousands of dwellings. Land had been progressively reclaimed from the lake by the ingenious use of *chinampas* or "floating gardens": the system consisted of clearing canals through the marshes and piling up the mud dredged from the canals to be held in place by retaining wickerwork frames. The resultant plots of land were then planted with crops and trees so that the roots bound the soil. An intricate network of canals divided the *chinampa* plots and served the dual purpose of transport and drainage. By this process, the original rocky island had been increased to an area of two square miles. Larger canals divided the city into four main zones or wards, each with its own temple precinct and market plaza. The neighbouring centre of Tlatelolco, once on a separate island, had become merged with the expanding metropolis. Lakeside suburbs were linked to the island by causeways, increasing the city's extent still further. Aqueducts supplied fresh water from springs at Chapultepec (literally "Grasshopper Hill") on the west shore, and from the district of Coyoacan in the south.

Temples abounded in the city. At the very centre, where the three great causeways met in a broad plaza, was the main temple complex. Here a huge, flat-topped, stone pyramid supported the twin shrines of Tlaloc, the rain god, and Huitzilopochtli, the Aztecs' own protector. Twenty thousand captives, it is said, were sacrificed during the dedication ceremonies that were held 32 years before the Spaniards arrived. Ranged round the pyramid were ranks of temples, palaces and shrines, as well as an aviary of rare birds and a zoo, where the animals were fed the torsos of sacrificial victims whose hearts had been offered to the gods. Here, Moctezuma's own two-storeyed, 300-room palace stood next to those of his predecessors. It contained luxurious apartments for himself, his two wives and numerous concubines; indoor pools and vast colonnaded halls housing courts of justice and central government offices; royal treasure hoards, workshops for master-craftsmen and quarters for the Emperor's 300 servants, his 200-strong guard of chieftains and his court entertainers— dancers, stilt-walkers, acrobats and jesting, humpbacked dwarfs.

Bernal Díaz records the Spaniards' first visit, with Moctezuma as their guide, to the main market-place in Tlatelolco. They were amazed at the largest commercial hub they had ever seen, a trading centre teeming with thousands of Indians who were bartering for slaves, precious stones, fabrics, pottery, timber, sweetmeats, feathers, axes, knives, tobacco, vegetables, medicinal herbs, ocelot skins and—unknown to Europeans then—chocolate and domesticated turkeys. But the wonder of the Spaniards soon turned to horror as they climbed the huge pyramid of Huitzilopochtli nearby and gazed on shrines that were, according to Díaz, so splashed and caked with human blood that the stench was worse than that of any slaughter-house in Spain.

The Spaniards were unspeakably shocked by the religious sacrifices they witnessed and they deeply alienated the Aztecs by their uncompromising criticism of the rites. Cortés himself even histrionically smashed some of the idols in their own temples. The Spaniards' avarice was another point of friction. The dream of gold had been one of the prime motives of the expedition; and although Cortés was careful to prevent any theft, his men could not conceal their lust for treasure, as the Mexicans sourly noted: "They picked up the gold and fingered it like monkeys: they seemed transported with joy, as if their hearts were illuminated and made new . . . they hungered like pigs for that gold." While seeking a place to build a chapel for themselves in the palace where they were quartered, the Spaniards broke through a plastered wall and discovered concealed there the Emperor's immense personal treasure of gold, silver, jewels and jade. They prudently walled it up again, but later prevailed upon Moctezuma to

A Violent History of Conquest and Revolutio

B.C.	c. 5000-2000	Domestication of maize in Mexico leads to gradu development of small Indian settlements
	c. 1000	Prosperous agricultural villages fringe Lake Texc in the Valley of Mexico
	c. 800	Influences of Olmec culture appear in the valley
A.D.	c. 200	City-state of Teotihuacan, located 30 miles from present-day Mexico City, is built. Over next 500 y it becomes the major religious centre of the so-c Classic Civilization that extends over much of Me
	c. 750	Teotihuacan is destroyed, probably by warlike nomads entering the valley from northern Mexico
	c. 900-1100	Waves of migratory Chichimec tribes from the n penetrate valley, establishing numerous city-stat
	1175	The Aztecs, last of the nomadic Chichimec peopl enter the valley
	1325	Aztecs settle on an island in Lake Texcoco, foun the city of Tenochtitlan
	1427-40	Aztecs begin to dominate neighbouring states
	1486-1502	During reign of warrior-emperor Ahuitzotl, Aztec empire spreads to its greatest extent, forcing mo of central Mexico into tribute-paying vassalage. Tenochtitlan, the capital, reaches height of splen
	1502	Devout, unwarlike Moctezuma II is elected Empe
	1519	Expedition of Spanish adventurers from Cuba, un Hernán Cortés, marches on Tenochtitlan. Profiti by Moctezuma's religious awe of the invaders, th take him hostage
	1520	Moctezuma II is killed while trying to keep peac Aztecs attack Spanish, forcing them to flee
	1521	With aid of Aztecs' rebellious Indian subjects, th Spanish return and destroy Tenochtitlan. On the s site they found Mexico City. Heavy influx of Spa colonists reduces native population to serfdom
	1527	Spanish royal decree establishes first Audiencia (commission) to govern colony of New Spain wi Mexico City as its capital. Friars undertake conversion of Indians to Catholicism, establishi lasting influence of the Church
	1553	University of Mexico City is founded
	1562	Cortés' original headquarters, renamed National Palace, becomes residence of Spanish viceroys
	1571	Spanish Inquisition is instituted in Mexico
	1608	Valley's first major drainage scheme undertaken
	1667	Cathedral of the Assumption is consecrated
	1692	National Palace is rebuilt after devastating fire
	1709	Church dedicated to Virgin of Guadalupe opens
	1783	Construction of Chapultepec Castle, intended as viceregal residence, begins
	1808	King Ferdinand VII of Spain yields throne to Jos Bonaparte. Creoles (those of Spanish blood but Mexican birth) seek independence from Spain
	1810	Father Miguel Hidalgo y Costilla musters a large peasant army and calls for redistribution of land, racial equality and independence
	1811	Hidalgo marches on Mexico City but draws back the last moment. He is captured and executed
	1815	José María Morelos, mestizo (mixed-blood) pries and disciple of Hidalgo who has continued the r in the southern provinces, is captured and execu His death marks temporary end of mass moveme for Mexican independence
	1821	Conservative forces of Church, army and landow in Mexico make temporary alliance with democr liberals to seize power in Mexico City. They decl Mexico independent under leadership of Creole General Agustín de Iturbide
	1822-23	Iturbide forfeits liberal support by his autocratic as Emperor Agustín I. The following year he is executed by liberal-dominated government
	1824	Newly convened Mexican Congress frames libera constitution setting up democratic, federal repu

hand it over to them—ostensibly as tribute to the King of Spain to whom the Aztec Emperor was persuaded to swear allegiance.

Moctezuma did his best to conciliate the two incompatible sides, but only succeeded in gradually forfeiting the trust of his people as he failed to control the behaviour of the uninvited guests. The crisis came when Cortés himself was absent from Tenochtitlan, forced to make a dash back to the coast to confront an expedition sent to attack him by his enemy Velázquez, Governor of Cuba. Cortés defeated the expedition, captured its commander and persuaded the troops to join him; but during his absence from the capital, his lieutenant had provoked violent reprisals by a senseless massacre of a group of unarmed nobles who were performing a ritual dance in honour of Tezcatlipoca. He returned to Tenochtitlan in time to re-enter the city with reinforcements of about 800, bringing the Spanish strength to over 1,200 men. Yet there was no doubt that they were doomed if they stayed in the city. In desperation, Cortés asked Moctezuma to seek a truce. Moctezuma knew that it was useless; yet still he climbed to the roof of the palace to plead with the angry crowds to make peace. The reply was a volley of arrows and stones. Three sling-stones struck his head. Three days later—presumably from his injuries, though some insist from a broken heart—he died.

On June 30, 1520, the Spaniards' final attempt at flight by night resulted in an apocalyptic massacre, in which all but 440 of them perished, some by drowning in the lake—dragged down by the weight of gold they carried —and some taken alive to have their hearts torn out at once in sacrifice to the gods they had outraged.

After this débâcle, referred to ever after as *La Noche Triste* (The Sad Night), the survivors—still led by Cortés, with his faithful Malinche—fled around the north shore of the lake, retreating a hundred miles eastwards to Tlaxcala. There, reunited with the implacable enemies of the Aztecs, they spent a further five and a half months preparing for a full-scale invasion of Tenochtitlan. Additional weaponry and gunpowder were brought inland from Veracruz. Thirteen stout, gun-carrying sloops were built to combat the thousands of Mexican dugout canoes. Reluctantly, but necessarily, Cortés accepted the Tlaxcalans' offer of 10,000 warriors; soon other tribes, including alienated allies of the Aztecs, began to throw in their lot with the Spaniards. Eventually, the total force that attacked Tenochtitlan probably numbered about 100,000.

Cortés' last campaign, brilliantly but ruthlessly executed, began on December 28, 1520. Before striking at the capital itself, he spent several months subduing neighbouring cities. Meanwhile, Tenochtitlan was ravaged by an epidemic of smallpox, deadliest of the weapons carried by the Spaniards. Thousands of Mexicans died, among them Cuitlahuac, Moctezuma's brother and successor, who had reigned for only 80 days. During the 16-week siege that began in April 1521, thousands more were to die from starvation. Encircling the city, Cortés controlled the causeways and destroyed the aqueducts to cut off food and water from the defenders.

This time there could be no surrender by the Mexican people. They were led resourcefully by a new warrior-emperor whose code was death before dishonour: the unyielding Cuauhtemoc (Falling Eagle), cousin and son-in-law of Moctezuma. Under his command, the city was heroically defended until—on August 13, 1521, after more than three months—the Spaniards overwhelmed the last centre of resistance, at Tlatelolco, in the northern sector of the city. Bernal Díaz del Castillo wrote, "We found the houses full of corpses, and some poor Mexicans still in them who could not move away. The city looked as if it had been ploughed up. The roots of any edible greenery had been dug out, boiled and eaten, and they had even cooked the bark of some of the trees. . . ."

Cuauhtemoc, seeking to escape by canoe, was captured by one of the Spanish sloops. On being brought before Cortés, the last Emperor of the Aztecs, about 24 years old, begged Cortés to kill him with his dagger. "I have done my duty," he said. His request was refused. And although Cortés embraced him and praised his courage, Cuauhtemoc was to be subjected to torture as the Spaniards tried to force him to reveal the whereabouts of his uncle Moctezuma's treasure, which had disappeared in the confusion of *La Noche Triste*.

This was the last war that the Aztecs and their subjects ever fought. Instead of simply losing their hegemony and having to pay tribute to a new overlord in a familiar world, they found their entire civilization ended forever. Only a tiny remnant of the population survived to see the change. It is estimated that between 1519 and 1607—through hunger, epidemics and exploitation—the native population of Mexico diminished by a staggering 95 per cent. Thus, Moctezuma's pagan fears were justified. The coming of Cortés did indeed presage the end of the Aztec world.

Most ancient cities have some surviving areas where you can feel directly the presence of history. But in Mexico City, the disappearance of every vestige of the Aztec city is almost complete—a strange contrast with the survival of detailed knowledge about what the city was like. That knowledge comes from a variety of sources, both Aztec and European. The Aztecs themselves were indefatigable bureaucrats, who kept voluminous accounts, annals, tax registers and other formal records, although their pictographic script did not allow more than a shorthand version of the facts recorded. Their literature of songs, hymns, poems and precepts was embodied in a rich oral tradition, passed on generation after generation. Only a few Aztec picture-writings have endured, hidden by Indians to preserve them; the rest were systematically burned by the Spaniards as blasphemous. But paradoxically the Conquest also contributed to the preservation of Aztec culture; with the arrival of the European alphabetic

In this illustration—a fragment of a 16th-Century Mexican manuscript—the Spanish adventurer Hernán Cortés (centre, left), leader of the expedition that conquered Mexico in 1521, receives gifts from Aztec nobles on his march towards Tenochtitlan. Malinche, his Indian mistress and adviser (below, centre), plays a crucial role as interpreter. Probably produced in the 1540s, the painting still uses some traditional Aztec stylistic devices.

The central Plaza de la Constitución—known simply as the Zócalo—is Mexico's largest public square. Dominated before the Conquest by the main Aztec

temples and palaces, the Zócalo now gains a distinctly Spanish character from the baroque cathedral (centre), and from the National Palace (right).

script, many Aztec traditions were written down for the first time, both in Nahuatl and in Spanish. Literate Indians recorded their oral traditions; and some Spaniards learned Nahuatl, made meticulous investigations, and wrote their findings in the Aztecs' own language.

In addition, there are the reports and narratives written by Europeans— notably the conquistadors themselves—about what they saw during and immediately after the Conquest. Fortunately for posterity, they had a strong sense of the historic drama they were creating and felt compelled by the very nature of their deeds to record them. They were explorers of the unknown and standard-bearers of Christian civilization. Besides, they often had a very real involvement in the strange world they discovered and an admiration for its achievements. All of Europe was their spellbound audience. When the artist Albrecht Dürer saw Moctezuma's offerings to Cortés, exhibited as early as 1520 in Belgium, he wrote in his journal, "I have seen nothing that has so rejoiced my heart as these things. For I saw in them strange and exquisitely worked objects and marvelled at the subtle genius of the men in distant lands."

These records have lost none of their power in the years since then. But the vivid mental pictures I had forged from the sources before I ever saw Mexico City had ill-prepared me for the fact that there are no areas within the city itself—like the Forum in Rome or the Acropolis in Athens—where buildings have weathered the centuries to offer visible reminders of Tenochtitlan. Recent governments have mounted ambitious excavations to make up for the lack, and you can find, for instance, the excavated foundations of a temple pyramid at Tlatelolco, now a district of Mexico City. The foundations, revealed and tidied up during slum clearance in the 1960s, are all that remains of the pyramid of Huitzilopochtli that so shocked Cortés and his companions on their first visit to the market-place. In a self-conscious allusion to the truncated pyramid, the neighbouring colonial Church of Santiago and surrounding modern buildings, the site is now called the Plaza of the Three Cultures.

The reason for the disappearance of the Aztec city for so many centuries is that Cortés set out, immediately after his victory, to supplant every trace of Aztec power, both material and spiritual. Demoralized by defeat and decimated by disease, the remnant of the nation was forced to demolish any buildings that had survived the catastrophic siege, and then to toil under the orders of their conquerors to construct an alien city out of the rubble. In four years, a new city—Ciudad Imperial de Mexico—had taken shape, and it was a very different shape from that of the Aztec capital. The houses and churches were thick-walled and small-windowed, fortified against possible uprising. Cortés, with the express purpose of preventing any Aztec revival, placed the administrative and religious headquarters of the Spanish colony directly upon the foundations of the corresponding Aztec buildings. His own palace (later used as the residence of the viceroys)

An 18th-Century painting by an unknown artist details the majestic splendour in which a Spanish viceroy journeyed by coach through Mexico City to hear mass at the cathedral. The canvas richly illustrates all the vigour and bustle of the Zócalo, then known as the Plaza Mayor, with its fashionably dressed crowds, and traders selling fruit and vegetables from covered stalls.

replaced Moctezuma's palace, and nearby a church was built on part of the site of the Great Teocalli. Rebuilt as the National Palace and the Cathedral of the Assumption, the institutions planted by Cortés still exist in the Zócalo.

The first rough-and-ready town built by the Spaniards soon gave way to an ordered, geometrically planned city, with fine houses and churches in a succession of European styles—which, however, took on a special Mexican flavour as interpreted by Mexican builders. Canals were filled in and streets widened, until the only relics of the original city were the place-names and main avenues that reflected the course of the great causeways. Lake Texcoco was partially drained to reclaim land—albeit very unstable land, as it has turned out since—and the valley and mountainsides were progressively denuded of their magnificent forests to provide timber for the colonists. The economy was transformed by new techniques of farming and mining, and the introduction of draught animals to replace human porterage. For the Indians, however, the story was one of ceaseless exploitation under one system or another, in spite of the earnest efforts of a few high-principled individuals, both churchmen and statesmen.

As the viceregal seat of government for 300 years, Mexico City saw 62 Spanish viceroys come and go. The centralized government of the Spanish colony perpetuated the centralism of the Aztec empire, ensuring that the city always far outstripped in size and influence any possible competitor. Ideas and controls were disseminated from it, and products flowed into it for transmission back to Spain. In the 17th Century, the city was not only the largest centre in New Spain, it was also the most lavishly wealthy.

Thomas Gage, an English traveller, was impressed to find in 1625 that even "tawny maids" wore "earbobs of considerable jewels".

The *mestizo* (mixed-blood) portion of the population gradually increased until it became an important element in the community, although lacking any real political recognition or rights. Meanwhile, colonial settlement expanded northwards and, by the end of the 18th Century, Mexico City found itself the administrative and political nucleus of a territory that extended from Guatemala to a line as far north as San Francisco—an area twice the size of modern Mexico, and over five times bigger than the Aztec empire. During the 18th Century, the streets of Mexico City were paved and lit, a police force was established, hospitals and prisons were modernized, delightful walks and *paseos* (carriage lanes) were laid out at the urban perimeter, and the viceregal palace and other buildings were "classicized" to suit contemporary taste.

But the tensions and conflicts within the city's complex racial and political hierarchy could not be contained forever. The mestizo population chafed at their lack of rights, and the Creoles—those of pure Spanish blood but colonial birth—resented the fact that all important government posts were filled by European Spaniards appointed by the Spanish Crown.

In 1808, during the wholesale European disturbance of the Napoleonic wars, a crisis in the Spanish monarchy brought to a head the stresses in Mexican society, and in 1810 a Creole rebellion broke out. Then, in the town of Dolores, about 150 miles north of Mexico City, Father Miguel Hidalgo y Costilla, a Creole village priest, rang his church bell and gave the now famous *grito* (cry): *"Mexicanos! Viva Mexico! Viva la Independencia!"* Fiery, intelligent and nationalistic, the priest drew behind him such an unexpectedly enormous "people's army" that he frightened the Creole and Spanish establishment into opposition against him. The tide of rebellion washed only as far as the outskirts of Mexico City and then receded; Hidalgo, himself probably appalled at the violence he had un-leashed, refused to let his army attack the capital. The Spanish viceroy strengthened his defences and, by 1811, Father Hidalgo had been captured and shot. Four years later the same fate befell his successor and disciple, a mestizo priest, Father José María Morelos.

Loyalty to Spain was apparently restored. But finally, in 1821, liberal reforms in Spain alienated the conservative Creoles because of implied threats to the revered institutions of Mexican life—chiefly the army and the Church. Under the leadership of a Creole militia officer, Agustín de Iturbide, Mexico became independent to avoid having to change its ways. Mexico City, a capital for 500 years, had a new nation to call its own.

By the time Mexico City became the capital of the present-day Mexican nation, it had already had two histories—one Indian and one Spanish. Anthropologists agree that modern Mexico is the result of a fusion of two old and diverse cultures and that it is this indissoluble mixture that gives

A defiant statue of Cuauhtemoc, the Aztec Emperor who led the final, gallant resistance to Cortés, commands a major intersection on the Paseo de la Reforma. Following Mexico's independence from Spain in 1821, newly fired nationalistic feeling led to the glorification of such native Mexican heroes.

This church bell, hanging outside the National Palace, is rung on September 15 each year to commemorate the outbreak of the Mexican War of Independence in 1810. The bell was brought to Mexico City from the church of Father Miguel Hidalgo y Costilla, the provincial priest who led the initial revolt against Spain.

Mexico—and Mexico City—its unique national character. It can be very difficult, if not impossible, to distinguish the proportions of Indian and Spanish blood that make up the Mexican mestizo. In any case, such an exercise is distasteful to the ordinary Mexican, who prefers to wipe clean the ancestral slate and be recognized as a new individual in his own right.

Nevertheless, the duality is there in the Mexican character and identity; and it is a subject of endless debate among observers of the country, and among Mexican intellectuals. If you look hard enough, you can find every shade of opinion, from those who think that the Aztecs were a godlike nation of erudition and wisdom brought low by the cynical exploitation of brutal Spaniards, to those who attribute all value to Spain's gift of European civilization bestowed upon a benighted land of bloodthirsty heathens.

Spain is, of course, historically important to Mexico, although relations between the modern states are not close. She has given Mexico her language and religion, and—broadly speaking—her cultural and intellectual traditions. At significant periods new ideas reached Mexico from Spain: anarchists and radicals arrived in the 19th Century, for example; and in the 1930s and 1940s refugees from the Spanish Civil War and from the Franco dictatorship—to which the Mexican government was extremely hostile—brought new life to Mexico's intellectual circles. Since the end of Franco's regime, Mexican-Spanish relations have been forged anew.

There are still about a million people who speak Nahuatl in Mexico, but the direct survival of Indian languages, customs and institutions is confined to rural areas and it plays no part in the life of Mexico City. Yet the philosophical and political weight given to Indian contributions to Mexican history seems to increase continually. Political rhetoric from the time of the Mexican Revolution in 1910 has continually invoked the Indian cause as the side of the angels and blackened the Spanish colonists as conscienceless exploiters. The great murals of Rivera, Siqueiros and Orozco that spell out this story date from the decades following the Revolution. The government operates according to much the same philosophy today, directing its educational policy towards an increased awareness of Indian elements in history and society, financing excavations and endowing museums.

And not without effect. There is a kind of grass-roots loyalty to the idea of the Aztecs as the original Mexicans and a consuming interest in any reminders of them. And even if all trace of Tenochtitlan has gone from the surface, history still lies beneath one's feet at every step—and in such abundance that any fresh excavations (as was shown spectacularly in the 1960s when the city's subway system was begun) are liable to yield a fresh hoard of Aztec relics. The most fruitful vein of Aztec riches runs beneath the old centre of Tenochtitlan, in the region of the Zócalo.

I remember vividly the first time I explored the Zócalo. I was heading for the cathedral when I was distracted by a noisy crowd converging on a street one block away to the north-east. There, everyone was pressing around a roped-off hole in the ground, a trench made by workmen who were installing electrical transformers. "Come on!" shouted one onlooker. "Give us our treasure! We pay our taxes and we want our share!"

What treasure? An immaculately dressed businessman, standing beside me in the crowd, explained that the workmen had recently uncovered a 20-ton ceremonial stone dedicated to an Aztec moon goddess called Coyolxauhqui, and now government archaeologists were excavating the site. "Who knows what they will find? Many people believe that Moctezuma's treasure was buried in these parts or else thrown into Lake Texcoco to keep it from the Spaniards."

He was referring to the golden hoard that Cortés' men had amassed in Tenochtitlan, only to lose it in their flight on *La Noche Triste*; and in Mexico City I was to hear many more references to Moctezuma's missing treasure. Even among poorly educated Mexicans, I was never to meet one who was not vaguely familiar with the story of how the Spaniards, in 1521, tortured young Cuauhtemoc to make him reveal where the treasure was hidden.

According to Bernal Díaz, the Emperor Cuauhtemoc and one of his lordly cousins "confessed" after their feet had been burned. Subsequently, he says, gold and jewels were fished out of a pond in the palace gardens. But who believes what a Spanish witness wrote more than 400 years ago? No true Mexican patriot can accept that story. Cuauhtemoc, leader of Mexico's first great resistance to foreign imperialists, has become a cult figure. Mexican history books now give a more prideful version of his life. He never "talked" or even screamed out in agony. His only utterance, they claim, was a reproof when his wailing cousin begged him to reveal the gold.

Later, in 1525, Cortés had the brave Cuauhtemoc hanged. He thereby gave the Mexican people their first true martyr; and it is held that the secret of Moctezuma's treasure went with him to the grave.

I asked the stranger beside me whether he believed there was any treasure. "It is possible," he replied. "But I don't think they will find it here." He paused and then grinned. "Have you heard the other version of what happened when Cuauhtemoc was tortured? Cortés kept asking him where they could find the gold. And Cuauhtemoc kept on telling him. But every time he told him, the interpreter invented a false translation so that he could keep the gold for himself. Maybe that's what happened. Another treacherous Malinche!"

Archaeologists never did find any treasure in those diggings north-east of the Zócalo, but they did unearth 300 Aztec artefacts: obsidian and jade knives, sea-shell necklaces and stone sculptures. No one was surprised. They were digging where once stood the Great Teocalli of Tenochtitlan.

It was in this area that the most fascinating of all Aztec relics was discovered in 1790: an enormous circular stone, more than 24 tons in weight, four feet thick, 12 feet in diameter and covered with mysterious symbols surrounding the solar face of the sun god Tonatiuh. This mono-

Outside the Museum of Mexico City, a child sits beside a cornerstone perhaps representing Quetzalcoatl, the all-powerful, plumed serpent god of the Aztecs. Probably once part of an Aztec temple and subsequently used by the 16th-Century Spaniards in their complete rebuilding of the city, the sculpture is one of the very few Aztec relics to have remained on view throughout the succeeding centuries.

lith of dark grey basalt is the famed Aztec Calendar Stone, so called because its diverse symbols define, among other things, the Aztecs' system of 18 months of 20 days in a year, and sacred cycles of 52 years. The stone is now the most familiar pre-Hispanic object in Mexico. Its complex pattern of concentric circles around strange hieroglyphics is stamped on billions of touristy souvenirs: leather goods, silver pendants, copper plates and wooden bowls; and the great disc itself is the most celebrated exhibit in Mexico City's National Museum of Anthropology.

It has found a fitting home. The National Museum of Anthropology, with all its stony-faced images of pagan gods, is the Great Teocalli of modern Mexico: a temple dedicated to the nation's pre-Hispanic cultures. Everything here is of monumental proportions. The museum's approach in Chapultepec Park is guarded by the largest monolith in the Americas: the solemn, imposing figure of Tlaloc, 23 feet tall and 168 tons of solid basalt. And, beyond him, the main entrance leads into an immense patio, half covered by an umbrella of concrete and steel, measuring 265 feet by 175 feet. Incredibly, and uniquely, this structure is supported by a single bronze-clad stone pillar subtly veiled by the cascading water from its built-in fountain. Altogether, the building is the most spectacular institution of its kind in the world, and more than 1.5 million people visit it every year. Opened in 1964, it has taken a secure position as one of the holy places of the nation.

I was drawn back to the museum again and again, simply because it so graphically represents the development of ancient Mexico, with its succession of pre-Columbian cultures—Olmec, Mixtec, Zapotec, Mayan, Toltec and finally Aztec. But I must confess—at the risk of being accused of sacrilege—that, to my mind, the museum does not allow history to speak for itself; rather, as an inscription on its dedication plaque makes clear, history is made to speak for a modern nation striving to establish a true identity of its own by exploring and pridefully proclaiming the achievements of its ancient forefathers. In pursuit of that aim, the museum has been chronologically arranged in such a way that it gives the all-too-neat impression of Mexican civilization steadily advancing to a pinnacle of achievement evinced by the shining island-city of Tenochtitlan.

Here we learn that the "flowering" of Aztec culture was the last great event in the history of pre-Hispanic Mexico. But the museum offers only the vaguest hints of the ruthless world that this flowering entailed. Of all its myriad and marvellous exhibits, few are more inconspicuous than a small, drum-shaped object labelled "Aztec sacrificial stone", and displayed with less notable relics in an obscurely positioned show-case. On that stone, Aztecs stretched out the living body of each sacrificial victim while a priest plunged in his obsidian knife and tore out a palpitating heart. I agree there is no reason why modern Mexicans should emphasize such medieval horrors. Equally there is no reason to exalt the Aztec period at the

In the central court of the National Museum of Anthropology, opened in 1964, a single pillar supports the world's largest cantilever roof, measuring 265 feet by 175 feet. The adjoining exhibition rooms are no less spectacular, presenting unrivalled collections of art and artefacts recording each of Mexico's numerous pre-Hispanic civilizations.

In the Museum of Anthropology, pupils study the astronomical symbols carved on Mexico's greatest Aztec relic: the 24-ton Calendar Stone.

expense of the whole historical truth. As the Mexican poet Octavio Paz has observed: "To enter the Museum of Anthropology is to penetrate an architecture built of the solemn matter of myth."

He is surely right. But this in itself is hardly surprising, since myth-making is the foremost industry of Mexico City. Here, more than in any other city I know, the people are prone to believe what they choose to believe, to ignore what they wish to ignore and to disguise fiction as fact whenever the mood so takes them.

When I first arrived in Mexico City I was astonished to hear some well-educated citizens insisting that it had never been proved that the Aztecs indulged in human sacrifices. Indian hieroglyphics, they argued, had been misinterpreted, and the horrific details of mass sacrifices recorded by Spanish witnesses could be dismissed as foreign propaganda designed to justify crimes against the people of Mexico. In the same way, the city has been adorned with countless monuments and memorials to Mexican leaders and Mexican achievements, while almost every trace of the con-quistadors has been expunged. The Conquest is something best forgotten.

The Paseo de la Reforma, a supremely handsome boulevard, provides perhaps the best introduction to the history that Mexico wishes to remem-ber and that which it chooses to forget. Much wider than the Champs-Élysées in Paris, on which it was modelled in the 1860s, it was originally called the Paseo de los Hombres Illustres (Avenue of Illustrious Men). Every member state of Mexico's Union of States was invited to adorn the new avenue with statues of its favourite sons. But those honoured states-men and soldiers, memorialized on both sides of Reforma, are now mainly forgotten. The truly famous monuments stand at the artery's major intersections, in the centre of huge traffic circles known as *glorietas*.

Who are the chosen few? Most importantly, Cuauhtemoc commands the main intersection with the Avenida Insurgentes. He is portrayed as a defiant warrior, his spear poised for throwing; and every August 21, the anniversary of his torture, Indians in full regalia dance in his shadow. The monument also pays tribute to Cuitlahuac, the Aztec Emperor who ruled for only 80 days before succumbing to smallpox. But there is no place on the Reforma for the infinitely more famous Moctezuma II, the Emperor who lamentably failed to resist foreign intervention.

Christopher Columbus, surprisingly enough, commands a central position in this show-piece street of Mexico City. He is acceptable as an explorer but only because he never set foot on Mexican soil or became involved with the Conquest. Much more surprising, however, is the monument at the next *glorieta* to the east: the bronze figure of a horseman depicted riding roughshod over the weapons of conquered Indians. This huge equestrian statue is always called simply *El Caballito* (The Little Horse)—nothing more. The rider, whom Mexicans choose to ignore, is

Charles IV, an idle, weak-willed King of Spain who abdicated in 1808 in favour of his son, Ferdinand VII. He is the only Spanish monarch privileged to have a memorial in Mexico City. A plaque at the monument's base apologizes for this sorry exception, explaining that it stands there, not out of any love for Spanish royalty, but because Mexico chooses to conserve an outstanding piece of art. *El Caballito*, connoisseurs agree, is the finest equestrian statue in the New World, though only because the horse is so impressively sculptured. If the 30-ton statue had not been cast in a single piece, the rider would surely have been unseated long ago.

Curiously, the insignificant Charles IV has had a far better fate than the conqueror of Mexico. During the War of Independence, hatred of the Spanish was so intense that the mortal remains of Hernán Cortés had to be removed from his tomb in the Church of Jesús Nazareno, three blocks south of the Zócalo, and hidden in the chapel wall of the adjoining hospital which Cortés had founded in 1528. Subsequently, all statues of Cortés were broken up. Much later his image did reappear—anything but heroic—in the murals erected in the early decades of this century. For example, Rivera's mural in the National Palace shows him as a grotesque, hunchbacked figure of demoniac aspect; and Orozco's in the Hospicio Cabañas depicts a sinister, apocalyptic automaton. Today, there is not a single monument to Cortés in Mexico City; his memory has been so successfully obscured that very few citizens can even tell you where he is buried. People do not know and, more significantly, they do not care.

When I visited the 16th-Century Church of the Hospital of Jesús Nazareno, a badly neglected structure standing roughly on the spot where Cortés had his first meeting with Moctezuma, the church was deserted except for a middle-aged caretaker who showed me a simple plaque on the north wall of the sacristy. It recorded that Hernán Cortés was reinterred here in June 1947. "Every day," the caretaker explained, "we get a few tourists asking to see the tomb. We also get a few Mexican visitors. But mostly they come to see our famous Orozco murals. Very often they leave without ever realizing that Cortés lies buried on one side of the main altar."

What irony! The greatest of all conquistadors, the Spaniard who first brought Christianity and the Spanish language to Mexico, is now eclipsed by one of the famous Mexican mural painters who lampooned him.

Small Services for a Modern Capital

At a maize stall in a city market, one woman fastens a bag of banknotes while her partner ties up corn husks in which tamales (stuffed pancakes) can be steamed.

Alongside the big stores, supermarkets and hamburger joints that increasingly give Mexico City an American look, many traditional forms of commerce still flourish. In the poorer areas, as well as in side-streets near the city centre, tiny grocery stores and bars cater to local clienteles. Little shops offer a wide range of services and products, and many of them specialize in a single business, such as the repair of domestic appliances or the sale of charcoal and wood for the many homes that have no other cooking fuel. In the city's markets, stallholders often sell only one kind of produce: onions, perhaps, or watermelons. In addition to these petty retailers, all competing for the tiniest niches in the urban economy, craftsmen in back-street workshops make and repair baskets, shoes or musical instruments, keeping alive artisan skills that have been passed down for generations.

At a shop in a working-class neighbourhood, a customer with her child buys a bucket of charcoal.

An elderly shopkeeper weighs a purchase in the small general store he has run for 50 years. The cramped premises are within a few blocks of the Zócalo.

A satisfied customer regales his companions in one of the city's pulquerías. These starkly fitted taprooms, which mostly refuse admission to women or allot them a separate room, serve only pulque—a coarse milky liquor made from fermented cactus sap and usually served from wooden barrels. Now generally confined to poorer neighbourhoods, pulquerías are losing ground to bars that sell beer and soft drinks.

Outside a repair shop named Casa de Petra (House of Petra), a young boy stops to admire the ample charms of a figure, with rolling pin and blender, representing a maid. Petra is a common first name for maids in Mexico City and this establishment directs its sales approach to them. The notice beneath the figure promises: "If Petra breaks it, the house of Petra repairs it."

A craftsman repairs a cesta, the wicker racket used to catch and throw balls in the game jai alai.

A new guitar takes shape in a one-man workshop near the Zócalo while a possible heir to the business studies the scores of instruments awaiting sale or repair.

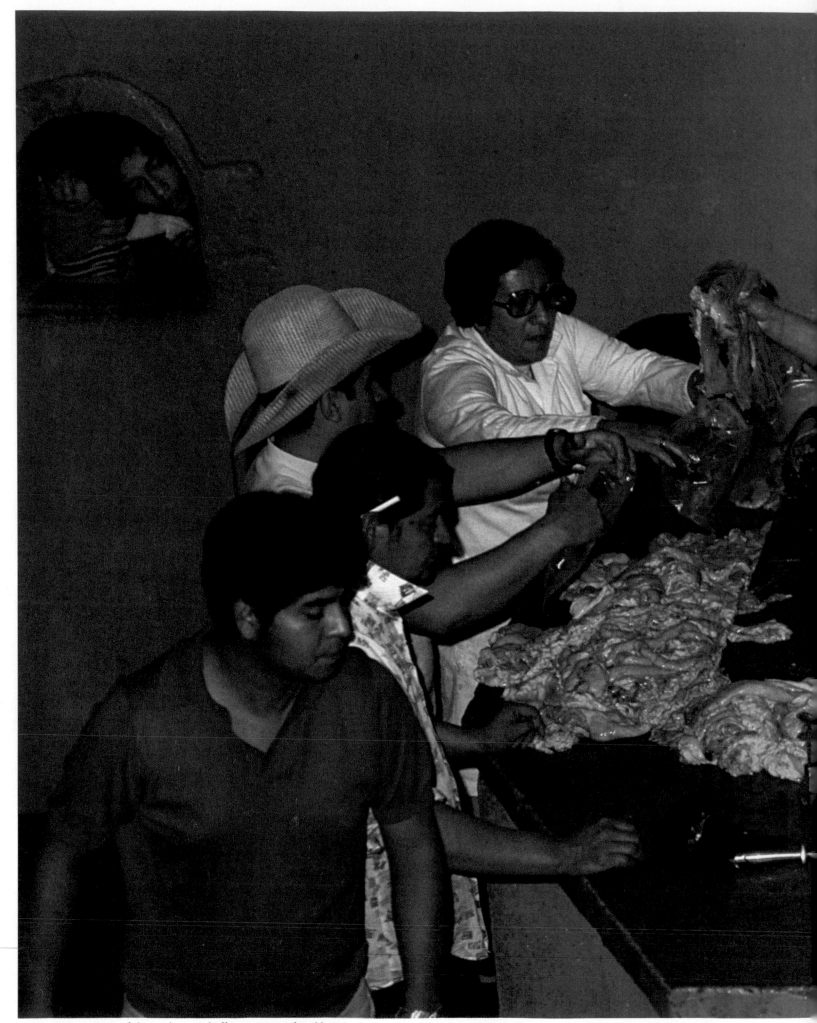

Within the precincts of the city's main bullring, a specialized butcher's shop does a brisk trade in cut-price beef offal, the by-products of an afternoon's sport.

3

Another Level of Life

Sooner or later anyone who gets to know Mexico City makes an illuminating discovery: it is not one city, but two. Or to be more precise, the city has two economies: one belonging to the sophisticated international world of industry, business, government and finance; the other consisting of a largely pre-industrial world of artisans and peasants, or *campesinos*, who are flooding into the city in search of a living. The people who inhabit one world have very little knowledge of the other. They secure their livelihoods by vastly different methods and organize their communities according to different conventions.

This division has been much accentuated by the so-called "Mexican miracle": the rapid industrialization that has more than doubled the gross national product since the end of the Second World War. Output first expanded during the war, both to satisfy increased demand in the United States for raw materials and manufactured goods, and to make up for the shortfall of imports in the domestic market. Since that time, Mexico's economic growth has continued at an average rate of 6 per cent a year, sustained by government and foreign investment in manufacturing and heavy industry, and by the development of the country's rich natural resources. In a few decades Mexico has made industrial strides that most developed nations took a century or more to achieve and the effects have, not surprisingly, been uneven.

The country's new prosperity and confidence was tellingly demonstrated in 1968 when Mexico City, at an outlay of $100 million, was able to tackle a challenge that almost all the great cities of the world are now reluctant to undertake: the staging of the Olympic Games. Enormous sums of money have also been spent on the capital's new housing developments, road-widening schemes, hospitals, highways and its ultra-modern Metro system. The proliferation of department stores, supermarkets, condominium apartments and American-style restaurants put up by commercial developers has transformed the life of the city.

But this new world has as many links with the international business community—especially the United States—as with the mass of the Mexican population. About half the 400 largest corporations in Mexico are foreign-owned, chiefly by U.S. companies; and there are more subsidiaries of major U.S. multinationals in Mexico than in any other Latin American country. Although extensive legislation exists to limit the level of foreign investment in Mexico, it is in many cases not strictly applied. In foreign-controlled companies, top policy-making posts—for instance

Rows of cave dwellings, many with front extensions, provide rent-free housing for the residents of Belén de las Flores (Bethlehem of the Flowers), a community that spreads over a terraced hillside not far from Chapultepec Park. Squatter settlements have mushroomed within Mexico City in recent decades, a symptom of the city's headlong growth from one and a half million to more than 13 million since the 1940s.

in technical and professional management—are often filled by non-Mexicans, or by Mexicans who have been trained abroad.

The proportion of Mexicans who participate directly in the thriving economy is strikingly low. A wealthy élite of industrialists, financiers, politicians, and high-ranking bureaucrats constitutes perhaps the top 3 or 4 per cent of the population. Beneath them is an urban middle class who belong to the country's best paid 20 to 30 per cent. The middle class takes its members from many groups, including the descendants of pre-revolutionary professionals and merchants; newly prosperous business-men and civil servants; and the technicians and skilled, unionized workers in the country's modern technological industries. Though widely differing, these groups have in common a consumer-orientated lifestyle that is still relatively new to Mexico City.

The far more populous and wholly Mexican world that exists alongside this affluence has very little share in it. Many of its people lack the basic literacy and skills necessary for industrial and technical work, and have little chance of finding steady jobs in the modern economy. The vast majority live either by casual labour or by working in one of the countless very small enterprises in the city. Many find jobs in little repair shops, retail businesses, garages or such long-established crafts as shoemaking. Others rely on one-man employments they have thought up for themselves: *taco*-seller, shoeshiner, grave-tidier, unofficial car park attendant or any other slight service that may earn them a few pesos.

The State provides no welfare amenities for the vast army of informally employed workers, who must rely instead on their own connections. Newly arrived *campesinos* usually join friends or relatives—even distant ones—who are already settled in the city and can help them get a footing. The resulting communities are often overcrowded, but they are tightly knit and preserve links with their places of origin.

In the late 1970s the expectation of increased revenue from Mexico's booming oil industry prompted renewed hopes that the gap between the two worlds would be narrowed. President José López Portillo acknow-ledged the desirability of giving a greater share of Mexico's increasing prosperity to the poor, when he proclaimed: "The time has come to end the traditional poverty that has been handed down from father to son as his only legacy. . . . It is grossly unfair to think of progress without con-sidering the jobless, the hungry, the sick, the ignorant and the homeless who can now be helped through benefits derived from the proper use of all our natural resources." It is easier said than done.

As a journalist observing Mexico City's great social divides, I was constantly struck by the gulf between the classes. They may live only a street apart and yet inhabit unrelated worlds. People dwell in caves only a few hundred yards from luxurious, three-million-peso mansions with electronically

Members of the exclusive Bosques de las Lomas ("Woody Hills") Racket Club enjoy an afternoon of tennis on courts built into a hillside next to a modern shopping centre. In Mexico City, where public courts are rare, tennis is strictly a sport for the affluent.

operated gates; the inhabitants of the tough and seedy streets of the inner-city district called Tepito live only a few blocks north of the National Palace and the Supreme Court.

Members of the wealthy élite work very hard—unlike the privileged in some other Latin American countries—and they gain enormous rewards. Their incomes originate in the affluent world of industry and international business, but they buy services cheaply from the pre-industrial world geared to the needs of the poor. They have access to superior private education for their children; the best medical attention (out of the city's 330 or more hospitals and clinics, three-quarters are small private establishments); membership of smart—and astonishingly expensive—golf, tennis and squash clubs; a social life that would be elegant by the standards of any capital in the world; holidays at whichever resort on Mexico's tropical sea coasts is currently the most fashionable; and the benefits of a weekend retreat, perhaps amid the bougainvillaea and jacaranda of salubrious Cuernavaca, a charming hill resort some 40 miles south and 2,000 feet below the capital. In spite of their constant and passionate complaints about the city's pollution and traffic congestion, the wealthy succeed remarkably well in preserving their own oases of comfort, order and refinement.

Mexico City's middle classes are in a quandary. As the first generation of Mexicans to bring up families in a stridently materialistic society, bombarded by enticements at every turn, they are caught between the two extremes of the city. They desire all the trappings of affluence and must compete for them with all who share their aspirations. They are constantly beset by worries: a bureaucracy that pours out a blizzard of application forms to be filled in for such things as driving permits, planning consents and business licences; the need to save up for the 30 per cent minimum down-payment required to buy a house or condominium apartment, and then to pay off the entire balance over the next 10 to 15 years at a very high rate of interest; the struggle to keep children at fee-paying schools rather than rely on the overloaded state system; the difficulties of securing satisfactory medical care; operating an automobile in a traffic-choked city where few drivers carry accident insurance; facing interminable delays when commuting by bus to and from the many areas of the city not served by the high-speed Metro.

Mexican life at the poverty level, I must confess, is a subject on which I had some vividly conceived notions when I first arrived in Mexico City. Like many foreigners, I had been profoundly impressed by the writings of the American anthropologist Oscar Lewis—in particular *The Children of Sánchez*, the classic work published in 1961 in which Lewis graphically reconstructed a family's life in the district of Tepito. The family lived in a *vecindad* (literally "neighbourhood"), a time-honoured institution of inner Mexico City. It can be defined as a self-contained slum tenement, one or sometimes two storeys high, usually built round a narrow courtyard behind shops facing on to the street. A small *vecindad* might accommodate as few as nine or 10 families; a large one may house several hundred people in numerous one-room apartments leading off a series of narrow court-yards. In his book, Lewis described a horrifying world of knife-fights, drunkenness, gambling, promiscuity and delinquency.

The Children of Sánchez is still widely read abroad, but it is resented by some Mexicans on the grounds that it gives foreign readers a picture of slum life in Mexico City that is exaggerated and outdated. Firstly, they argue, Tepito itself is by no means as forbidding as it was in the Fifties, when Lewis did his research. As the city has grown more prosperous, conditions in the area have improved. Secondly, say the critics, Tepito is no longer typical, since most slum-dwellers today are housed in makeshift shanty-town settlements on the city's periphery. They are absolutely right on both counts. But when it comes to describing the quality of life in very poor areas, they are at a loss.

One soon discovers that most residents of Mexico City are only too glad to keep away from such areas if they do not live there. Lacking first-hand knowledge, they are seized by fear of the unknown. I had a convincing demonstration of this rarely admitted truth when I took a taxi ride one day. I asked the driver to make a detour so that I could see a cave-dwellers' settlement in a neighbourhood picturesquely called Belén de las Flores (Bethlehem of the Flowers), located directly south of the wealthy hillside district of Las Lomas de Chapultepec, not far from the park. After crossing the Avenida Constituyentes, he turned and parked on the side of a steep

Children of several neighbouring families enjoy a communal scrub-down in the courtyard of a vecindad—one of the inner city's old slum-tenement complexes.

hill. Below us, on the far side of the valley, we could look down on rows of caves ranged along seven levels of the steeply terraced hillside. A community of about a thousand people lived here. All the caves had fitted doorways, some had one-storey extensions built out from the cliff, and many possessed a television aerial wired to a bamboo pole. A few pigs, goats and chickens roamed the surrounding slopes. I asked the driver to turn off down the earth track leading to the settlement. He refused, even after the offer of a tip. It was too dangerous, he insisted; people did not welcome strangers in this area; we were liable to be robbed or, at the very least, his car would be vandalized. He drove on.

Some weeks later I persuaded a friend to drive me out to the caves. Not wishing to appear as nosy intruders—which indeed we were—we went from cave to cave on the pretext that we were looking for a girl called Margarita who, we understood, might be available for work as a maid. To our shame, this subterfuge proved to be totally unnecessary; the troglodytes of Belén de las Flores were a warm and hospitable people, only too willing to talk to strangers and ask us in. Most of the caves were not more than about 10 feet deep. The rock walls were painted in bright colours, most often turquoise or blue. Some of the larger caves were divided into two small rooms by brick partitions; most were adequately furnished and fitted with electric lights. Outside some of the caves were small, carefully tended vegetable plots. One main tap provided municipal water for each terraced row of caves. There was a nearby general store and on the hilltop directly above stood a small school.

I asked several people if they would prefer to live elsewhere. Not one wished to move. Here they had a close-knit community, not too large, not too small, where they all knew their neighbours. They were near the city's main amenities, especially Chapultepec Park, but they did not suffer from the overcrowding of the inner city and their expenses were modest. "The government lets us stay here rent-free. We pay only for electricity and water," said one woman. "We have the best roof in the world because, even if it rains very hard, the water never seeps through the rock above." The cave-dwellers, I have since concluded, are among the more fortunate of Mexico City's low-income families, except in one important regard: there is no guarantee that they will not one day be evicted to make way for a development scheme. Such is the pressure on land in the city that almost every open space is sooner or later surveyed as a possible building site.

About half a mile below the caves, as we continued driving south, I saw an unusual sight: several hundred people gathered on a dusty slope of vacant land, preparing to hold a fiesta. It was a weekday of no national or religious significance; so why, I asked, were they having a fiesta? They explained that it was a Building Day Fiesta—a party for families who were being evicted from their nearby shanty homes because the land they had been occupying as squatters was required for a new bus terminal. These

A house in the wealthy district of Polanco, just north of Chapultepec Park, reflects in its ornate wrought-iron gateway and cumbersome stone arches the neo-colonial Hispanic style that pleased many of Mexico's moneyed entrepreneurs early in the 20th Century.

families were not entitled to any compensation, but they were receiving something they considered of far greater value: the authorities had given them legal possession of this vacant lot, free of charge. Today they were marking out their plots and celebrating. Tomorrow, as members of a co-operative association, they would start building. They would undertake all the construction work in their spare time; by pooling their resources and obtaining a modest bank loan they could buy materials such as cement and concrete blocks in bulk at reduced prices.

Controlling the growth of squatter settlements is one of the most intractable problems facing the authorities. The settlements suddenly appear from nowhere, a characteristic that has gained them the name *colonias paracaidistas* (parachutist colonies). The other name by which they are known—"lost cities"—equally well encapsulates the sense of hopelessness that clings to them and the difficulty of finding the way to them. Most of them are established at the outer edges of the city, on land not yet built up; some occupy ground nearer the centre that is unsuitable for conventional development because of topographical disadvantages such as unstable subsoil.

The authorities used to try to displace the illegal settlers by driving them off; but since no alternative sites were offered after an eviction it was impossible to stop the homeless from taking up possession once more. Hence the policy that successive governments have adopted since the mid-Sixties: acquiescing to and sometimes even assisting in the improvement of established squatter settlements. If the land is government-owned, the authorities may simply give it away to the squatters; if it is privately owned, the government can obtain it by compulsory purchase and sell it to the squatters at a nominal fee.

In this way the authorities get help from the homeless themselves in solving the city's housing problem. Once established, the former squatters must start paying land taxes and contributing to the cost of paving the streets and the supply of water. Illegal settlements can thus begin the transformation into self-respecting suburbs.

I gained my first introduction to life in one of the "lost cities" through a young couple, Roberto and Guadalupe Donadi. Both the Donadis had been students of English, and were already finding enough spare-time work teaching and translating to maintain a modest two-room flat off Reforma, run a Volkswagen "Beetle" and have a cleaning lady in once a week. Roberto, Argentinian-born, had travelled widely during two years' national service in the merchant navy. Guadalupe, a classic Mexican beauty, had lived for a time with an aunt in New York. Although middle class, they were a refreshingly unconventional pair whose genuine friendliness made them ignore Mexico City's social divides. They were on good terms with their cleaning lady and her neighbours, who lived on the out-

Unskilled labourers dig foundations for a new building. The city's booming construction industry attracts large numbers of migrants from rural areas.

skirts of Jalaitepito, a semi-developed area in the south-west of the city. One day they were invited over to visit the maid's neighbours—a family named Ramirez. Roberto asked me along "for a ride"—and what an inordinately long ride it proved to be! It brought home to me the sheer size and confusion of the Mexico City no tourist sees.

A map is virtually useless on a journey into the city's uncharted quarters. Roberto had made the trip once before; even so, when we reached the part of Jalaitepito we were making for, we needed to stop at least a dozen times to ask the way before we found the house. We were lost in a jumble of unpaved streets without names and without numbers; "asking the way" meant repeatedly asking strangers whether they happened to know the family we were looking for and where they lived. At the time of our visit this settlement was still in the embryonic stage. It contained 200 or so dwellings grouped randomly on one side of a disused gravel pit. To approach the Ramirez' house, we had to climb over banks of soil thrown up from a ditch that had been dug for main drains. A street was to be laid over it.

We eventually reached a small house, built of grey brick and cement, high on the slopes of the gravel pit. Three generations of the Ramirez family—who had moved a few years before from a country area near Guadalajara, Mexico's second largest city—were living in the house: 60-year-old Fidel and his wife Nina, their son Fernando and daughter-in-law Margarita, and three little grandchildren. Lodging with them was Fernando's cousin Manuel and his wife Lupita, plus Carmen, a 23-year-old single woman and her baby son, who had been homeless until taken into the family—11 people in all. Fidel and Fernando had built the house themselves. It had two rooms, each 12 feet square, a sloping roof of corrugated asbestos and a low-walled backyard that served as the outdoor kitchen. Followed by a free-roaming chicken, we entered the main room, which doubled as living-room for the whole family and bedroom for Fernando and Margarita and their three children. The other room was the bedroom for the remaining six occupants of the house. The centre of the living-room was occupied by a long table. Against the far wall stood a large television set and a radio-cassette-player. On the left of the doorway was a large double bed for Fernando and Margarita and their two older children. A hammock for the baby was suspended directly above. The remaining space was occupied by dining chairs, a wardrobe, a dresser and a refrigerator. On the walls and dresser were white-wedding photographs, pictures of the children and of Fernando with his local soccer team.

Fidel told us that when the family first arrived in Mexico City, they had built a small house above an obsolete sand-mine, but that property had been condemned by a government inspector because of its insecure foundations. A year ago they had resettled here. The new house had been given a postal number, we were told. But neither Fidel nor his wife—both illiterate, like so many of Mexico's poor—could remember the number, or even the name of the administrative district in which they lived.

Both Fidel and Fernando were casual labourers who did bricklaying and carpentry whenever work was available. They belonged to the army of workers employed in the city's booming construction industry. Sometimes, they claimed, they could each earn up to 1,500 pesos (about $70) in a week; often they were unemployed for months at a stretch, since the labour supply far outstrips the demand. Possibly they were exaggerating their earnings for my benefit, but per capita income in Mexico City is the highest in the country, in spite of the number of low-income families that daily swell the population; and the abundance of consumer goods in the Ramirez house was evidence of a relatively comfortable lifestyle. Many squatters manage to accumulate savings that tide them over bad patches and enable them to meet unexpected expenses.

Whenever *paracaidistas* descend on a vacant piece of land, the first service to be provided is electricity. Usually the squatters start by pirating the nearest supply, making their own connections to the municipal cables. Once a sizeable settlement has grown up, the residents often apply to the government for improved services to be provided officially. Because of the water shortage and awkward terrain, water and drainage may not be available for months, or even years, after the electricity.

When I asked Fidel why, after a year, they had still not added a third room, he explained that two rooms were quite enough trouble and expense. When you have no legal entitlement to the land and may be evicted at any time, there is little inducement to go beyond the minimum investment of money and effort. To make matters worse, the insecurity of squatters is sometimes exploited by people who pose as government officials and demand money for title deeds that never existed. "When we arrived here, a well-dressed lady came round to say that we could buy our building plot for 3,000 pesos. She took our money, but she didn't give us any papers and we never saw or heard from her again. It was the same with other families. Anyway, we built the first room. Then government officials arrived and charged us and the neighbours 7,000 pesos for levelling the surrounding land with a machine. They put in electricity and now we are going to have drains and water-pipes—all for small easy payments. We have receipts for money paid to the municipal authorities, but we still don't have any papers to show that we own the land."

As we left, I asked Fidel if he had any wish to move elsewhere. "No," he said. "Things are not too bad here. We can get a fair amount of building work and the water supply will be put in quite soon."

I had been in Mexico City less than a week when I first heard the name "Santa Fé". A business executive in his office on Reforma was complaining about the pollution. "It's disgraceful," he said. "They're burning

Mexicans queue to hand over valuables at the National Pawnshop (above), a state institution that enables the poor to borrow money at low interest rates on the security of personal items. In a showroom (right) three women inspect a variety of pawned objects that were not redeemed within the prescribed time limits and have thus been placed on sale.

the garbage out at Santa Fé again, and the smoke and soot are billowing all over the city. It shouldn't be allowed." Several weeks later I heard a maid telling her employers how, with several other women, she had gone to watch her husband playing in a minor league soccer match at Santa Fé. "The smell was terrible," she said. "We held our noses at first, but the local people looked so offended that we stopped. Soon afterwards, my friend started vomiting. I shall never go to that dreadful place again." The businessman and the maid were referring not to the district of Santa Fé, about seven miles south-west of the Zócalo, but to the municipal rubbish dump on its outskirts.

My reaction on seeing Santa Fé's "valley of garbage" for the first time was disbelief more than horror. The "valley" is actually a disused quarry more than half a mile across, excavated on high outlying ground. Through bushes lining the main road above, I looked down on a village community set amid mountains of stinking refuse that fouled the air far beyond the valley. Dogs, pigs, goats, sheep, chickens, even a few cows were scavenging in the garbage—alongside men, women and children who were busily sorting out bottles, rags, metalware and other re-usable items that might be sold for a few pesos.

For these people, the valley was work-place, home and recreation ground. From the main entrance, a sloping road provided access for garbage trucks. It led down the middle of the quarry, dividing it into two sections, each of which had its own grassless soccer pitch. A few families occupied a single row of prefabricated wooden shacks to one side of the site. The vast majority, perhaps a thousand or more, lived in scattered *jacales* and huts constructed of tin boxes, sheets of cardboard and scraps of

wood, erected both in and around the garbage. At the main gate a large notice declared: "It is forbidden for anyone to enter here if they are not concerned with the work."

Several weeks later I returned to the valley of garbage, intending to find out more about the life of this extraordinary community. This time I had much needed moral support from Roberto Donadi. Following our visit to Jalaitepito, Roberto had willingly driven me around a number of Mexico City's seedier quarters; but on this occasion he was less than enthusiastic. However, he could not resist a challenge and finally consented to go. We agreed that our pretext would be that we were scouting for football talent.

Once inside the valley, we attempted to look as casual and inconspicuous as possible, slouching along with never a hint of the revulsion that the indescribably foul smells were arousing within us. Somehow it didn't work. Almost at once, we attracted a group of ragged young Mexicans. Disturbingly, they said nothing—simply stood around, staring at us. They ignored our initial pleasantries, but at the mention of soccer, their attitude changed miraculously. They began to ask questions. Who did we think would win the next World Cup? Had we ever seen Pelé? What had gone wrong with English soccer? They were friendly and articulate, yet any attempt on our part to elicit information about their living and working conditions instantly revived their frosty looks.

One man eventually told us: "We have to work here because there are not enough unskilled jobs elsewhere. In the beginning I thought the smell was awful. But you get used to it. You can get used to anything in time. Now I don't think it's so bad. Here I can earn something every day. We can live pretty well." As he spoke, a pack of yapping mongrels ran by. "They help to keep the rats down," he explained.

By now we wanted to get away as far as possible from the nauseating, suffocating stench of rotting waste. As we started up the dirt track leading from the valley, we were surprised to meet a distinguished-looking lady, so smartly dressed that she would not have looked out of place at a presidential reception at the National Palace. Under her arm she carried a beginner's reading book. The lady, Señora Luz María Ituarte de Contro, was in her sixties. She told us that she was a banquet-organizer by profession. In her spare time she worked with a team of volunteers organized by her daughter, a nun, who visited depressed areas of Mexico City to teach adults basic literacy.

By way of this chance encounter I was to meet her daughter. Sister María del Carmen Contro Ituarte was headmistress of a large primary school and for years she had been visiting the dump one day a week to give free lessons. She told me a little more about the valley and its inhabitants, and her own feelings about them.

"The first thing that struck me there was the fact that all living things—pigs, turkeys, hens, rats and human beings—were existing on the same

Residents of the Santa Fé rubbish dump in south-west Mexico City sort through garbage for resaleable items. Nearby, their sheep, goats and pigs scavenge for scraps of food. The sorters live with their families beside the mounds of garbage in huts made of flattened jerrycans, wooden boxes and cardboard.

level. They were all collecting things from the garbage, all making a living out of the waste. It was man degraded to the very bottom of human dignity.

"I remember one day that a small child came to me and asked: 'Ma'am, is it true that rats turn into bats? There are lots of rats here and I've been told that they will grow wings and suck blood. But I don't believe it because the other night, when I was sleeping, a rat fell on my face and bit my nose. I grabbed it and threw it against the wall. The next morning I saw the dead rat and it didn't have wings at all.'

"Some of the children are lucky enough to attend classes in a small school at the entrance to the dump. But most of them have to work in the garbage whenever they are needed; just like everyone else, their families need the money. There are many illnesses in the dump, especially eye infections, gastro-enteritis and digestive problems. It is no wonder. After all, the most appreciated garbage trucks are those that bring leftover food from the supermarkets—rotting meat and vegetables that the people eagerly collect for their own nourishment.

"Some people say the dump is run by a trade union. But that's a lie. It would be better if there were a union. Instead, one boss controls everything there. He holds the concession to run the dump. Only he is allowed to sell things outside. And he is a millionaire. He makes a fortune out of the miserable business.

"I wanted to make a short film about these people in order to show the kind of problems they face. But the officials would not let me go into the dump with a camera. It was a shame because my only purpose was to create awareness among people, to show that their brothers are living in subhuman conditions, buried in the rubbish that we throw away.

"It is extraordinary. If you ask people if they would like to leave this horrible place and live somewhere else, they reply: 'Oh, no. We have a steady income here. We know that if we go and pick up some salvage, we can sell it immediately and get money—just a few pesos, but enough for beans and *tortillas* for the day.' Moreover, as they explain, they don't have to pay rent and they get a free ration of water provided by the authorities —two five-gallon cans for each family per week."

The valley of garbage is a particularly dramatic example of slum life in Mexico City and I would not wish to imply that it is typical. But then neither is it the lowest level of poverty in the city. There are other *jacale*-dwellers who are not even provided with a meagre water ration or a sure means of earning a few pesos. The significance of the Santa Fé rubbish dump lies not in its poverty or even its filth and degradation, but in the fact that Mexican society appears to tolerate such conditions and even allows them to be a source of profit.

I have watched the garbage-sorters delivering their bundles of scrap-metal and other saleable items to the "pit-head" weighing-machine at the main entrance of the Santa Fé garbage dump. They have to accept whatever the officials of the concessionaire choose to pay them for their finds. Whether or not the concessionaire has become a millionaire, as Sister María del Carmen claimed, I never managed to discover. But I have heard the same story from other reliable sources and I do not doubt that there is a truth behind it somewhere.

As every visitor to Mexico City knows, the Aztecs are still very effectively punishing foreign intruders by way of that peculiarly virulent form of gastro-enteritis known as "Moctezuma's Revenge"—or, less colourfully, as *turista*. The affliction, transmitted by unpurified water or over-handled food, is disastrous for tourists who have had no chance to build up an immunity. Shortly after my arrival in the city, an American businessman told me with some pride that he had visited Mexico City many times without suffering even a twinge of Moctezuma's Revenge. The secret, he said, was quite simple: "I never drink the water and I never eat outside my hotel." I ignored his dull formula for gastric stability, choosing instead to enjoy the variety of Mexican cuisine. Of course, I paid the price—and very unpleasant it was for more than a week. However, the condition is really of no lasting importance; you soon build up a resistance to it if you live in the city for any period of time.

Far more significant, in my view, is a sickness that threatens all the city's residents, foreigners and nationals alike. It is a condition of endemic proportions; yet it does not afflict any particular part of the body and apparently it has no cure. It is the disease of cynicism: a deep-rooted, self-diminishing, sceptical disbelief in the possibility of improvement. It takes root the moment one realizes the proportions of the city's problems and begins to explore all the reasons—political, practical and psychological—why their continuation seems inevitable. I have never been one of Mexico City's long-term residents; but as a writer on social and economic conditions, I was perhaps even more exposed than they to the germs of disenchantment. Just as with Moctezuma's Revenge, I suffered a sharp and painful attack. I can see, looking back, that it was no less inevitable.

The more I learnt of the problems facing Mexico City—overpopulation, unemployment, pollution, traffic congestion, exploitation of the poor—the less I could believe in the possibility of real change for the better. Encouraging though it is, the prospect of substantial wealth from Mexico's natural resources offers no magically prompt solutions. Some Jeremiahs argue that Mexico City is doomed to ultimate chaos whether new wealth is channelled into the city or not. If the government does not finance a massive development programme—bigger housing schemes, better transport facilities, increased water supplies, a proper sewage system—life in the capital will eventually become intolerable for everyone. Conversely, they continue, if such a programme is carried out, the city will simply attract still more migrants from depressed rural areas.

Women cluster round a congregant emerging
from the Church of San Juan de Dios in Santa
Veracruz Plaza. Taking advantage of an old
tradition of almsgiving in honour of St. Anthony
of Padua, whose much revered image is in the
church, poor women gather to beg on the steps
every Tuesday during a 13-week period leading
up to the saint's feast-day on June 13.

It is difficult to fault this gloomiest of arguments. During the 1960s the
truly impressive civic improvements made by the government were
quickly cancelled out. As better roads enabled more citizens to become
motorists, pollution and traffic congestion increased; as new industries
encouraged more *campesinos* to come into the capital in search of work,
overcrowding and housing shortages became more acute. The same
trends continued unabated during the 1970s: the Metro was extended,
more water was provided at appalling cost, pumped up from as much as
2,000 feet below the level of the city's mountain plateau; every year a few
more sprawling shanty towns were converted into properly serviced
suburban communities. But in that decade the population of the city more
than doubled; civic development simply could not keep pace.

One possible solution has long been recognized by successive administration: decentralization. On my last visit to Mexico City I had the good
fortune to be granted an interview by President José López Portillo.
During a flight to Guadalajara, on board his presidential airliner Quetzalcoatl II, he told me: "The extraordinary growth of Mexico City is the
result of the absence of a national development plan. We think it is
absolutely necessary to check the growth. But the supposition that it can
be checked with measures taken in the city itself—which would have to
be very dramatic measures—is just an illusion. The problem has to be
solved in the entire country, not just in the city."

The policy of decentralization, though frequently advocated, has never
been pursued on the scale required for success. Under the Portillo
administration, massive tax incentives were offered to industries willing to

leave the city. Companies failed to respond in any number because they had no wish to move away from vital markets and services, and into undeveloped areas. As one industrialist said to me: "What use are massive tax reliefs and far cheaper water if, to obtain them, we have to move to rural areas where services are inadequate for our production needs and we have the enormous added expense of transporting our goods back to the principal market-place—Mexico City?"

Mexico City's condition demands a more drastic solution. The real answer, it has been suggested, is to abandon major improvements to the capital, concentrate civil expenditure on the infrastructure of new cities outside the Valley of Mexico, and introduce a programme of compulsory emigration, moving out industries and workers en masse. But this, say the sceptics, plausibly enough, will never happen.

For one thing, the political system is an obstacle to long-term planning. Under the Mexican constitution, the entire ruling élite changes at the end of each six-year presidential term: not only the President and his ministers; but thousands of elected and appointed officials, from high-court judges and directors of state industries to the mayor of Mexico City. The system inevitably leads to a loss of continuity. Good intentions abound during the first two years of a presidential term; some progress may be made during the next two years; but the last two are so dominated by the question of who is to be the next President that the urgency goes out of any current improvement projects. Understandably, the succeeding President is unlikely to give priority to completing his predecessor's plans; he usually prefers to start his own attractive projects.

Vested interests and personal influence at different levels of society can be even more effective at blocking solutions. As long ago as March, 1971, sensible anti-pollution legislation was introduced, and yet it has never had any significant effect. A factory-owner may still find it more economical to pay a bribe—universally known as *mordida* (bite)—to an inspector than to install legally required purifying equipment. A motorist may risk driving his car without legally required exhaust suppressants in the knowledge that a bribe will probably enable him to escape a heavy fine. As for Mexico City's worst polluters—the thousands of privately owned buses that burn low-grade fuel and billow a black trail of diesel smoke—well, as everyone knows, they are virtually a law unto themselves. Indeed, the bus companies are so well protected by a so-called "mafia of lawyers" that ordinary citizens fatalistically accept that it is useless to sue one of them for damages in the event of an accident. All things considered, cynicism begins to seem like the only rational attitude.

Cynicism, though it feeds naturally on Mexico City's problems, was well established in the Mexican character before those problems had taken their present form. Engrained in successive generations, it manifests itself

A tiled tomb commemorates Conchita Jurado, an eccentric Mexican woman whose brilliant male impersonations in the 1920s gulled Mexico City's high society into believing she was an influential Spanish millionaire by the name of Don Carlos Balmori. Don Carlos' mustachioed image appears on the tomb's sloping top below Conchita's own spinsterish portrait. Painted tiles on the sides depict some of her hoaxes.

in many ways, including the Mexican gift for myth-making. This talent far transcends logic and reasonableness; it is instinctive—an integral part of a game of life in which people are free to give out their own edited version of the facts and equally free to discount other people's versions. The disregard for truth is displayed in the extravagant rhetoric of machismo—perhaps best defined as the boasting of competitively masculine individuals, who cannot possibly live up to their own images in real life; in the "revolutionary" stance adopted by what is really a conservative government; in the belief, connived at by a large proportion of the population, that the present-day Mexican state is the direct heir to the Aztec world and owes little to its Spanish heritage; and, at a much more practical level, in the claim of many single mothers that their husbands were bricklayers killed falling from high buildings, or else the victims of road accidents.

"Do you ever play outside the city?" I once asked a *mariachi*. Without anything to gain (I had already paid for his services), he gave me a long-drawn-out account of his tours of the United States and the Caribbean, and started listing all the great cities he had seen: Houston, St. Louis, San Francisco, Kingston, Havana. But another *mariachi*, who was not to be upstaged, gave a wink and continued the recital with compromisingly local names: "And Xochimilco, Tlalpan, Coyoacan, San Angel . . .". The globe-trotting *mariachi*, it emerged, had never travelled further than Guadalajara.

One of the most startling pieces of gratuitous invention I came upon—too extravagant to be typical, yet appropriate to certain moods of Mexico City—is the story of Concepción ("Conchita") Jurado, born in the city in 1865. As a young woman she invented an amazingly effective deception by impersonating a swaggering Spanish multimillionaire, absurdly masculine in every respect, whom she called Don Carlos Balmori. For years, Conchita's hoax remained an innocent party piece to be practised on relatives and close friends. But gradually the masquerade became more elaborate and daring until, in the mid-1920s when Conchita was nearly 60, it captured the imagination of a Mexican politician. He and a few influential friends, including a prominent newspaper-owner, decided the impersonation deserved to be played on a more ambitious scale.

With their backing, Don Carlos emerged in public. His financial coups, big-game hunting exploits and amorous adventures around the world were regularly reported, complete with pictures, in the Mexican Press. In time, everyone in Mexico City had heard of Don Carlos Balmori, the eccentric tycoon. And whenever one of his "visits" from Spain was reported, it raised the pulse of hordes of fortune-hunters—women aspiring to win the world's most eligible bachelor, businessmen eager to secure his financial support.

Conchita was a plain-looking mouse of a woman, soft-spoken, virtuous and retiring. But once she donned the mantle of Don Carlos and exercised her extraordinary gift for mimicry, she became the reverse of her own self—ostentatious, bombastic, unfeeling. Her carefully planned hoaxes were designed not merely to entertain, but to demonstrate the truth of her cynical claims that Mexicans will sacrifice virtually anything—honour, loyalty, love, self-respect—if only the price is high enough. In proving this point, she was horrifyingly successful.

The procedure was for new victims—selected from the upper echelons of Mexican society by Conchita's rich friends and known as *nuevos puercos* (new pigs)—to be introduced to the great Don Carlos Balmori at carefully staged social gatherings called *balmoreadas*. The victims—hundreds of them—were encouraged to think that Don Carlos might give or lend large sums of money for some project or other, but only if certain humiliating conditions were fulfilled.

A much decorated general, on promise of a cheque from the millionaire, was persuaded to part with his cherished medals for gallantry. A well-known industrialist, seeking finance for a new factory, agreed to Don Carlos' strange condition that he get down on all fours and roar like a lion. Dozens of women, too, were deceived by the pretended advances of Don Carlos and over-eagerly agreed to marriage. A famous detective, Valente Quintana, accepted a commission to protect Don Carlos from an old enemy who was said to be a master of disguises. Quintana assured Don Carlos that he would be absolutely safe because he could see through any disguise—at which point Conchita threw off her disguise and all the onlookers split their sides laughing. And each time she unmasked herself, Conchita ceremoniously stated: "Nothing is *exactly as it seems to be*. Nothing is real. The truth is always hidden."

After each *balmoreada*, the victim was sworn to secrecy and enrolled in Los Balmori, the most exclusive society in Mexico City, whose members could share in the masquerades and nominate victims. In reality it was more often pathetic than funny—a game taken to such extremes that it became downright heartless and cruel. Yet when Conchita died in 1931 at the age of 66, and the truth about Don Carlos Balmori was finally revealed to the public, it was greeted with delighted amusement; and one year later, on the anniversary of her death, more than 3,000 people gathered at her grave to commemorate her.

Like Conchita's hoax, Mexican history as far back as you look has been downright heartless and cruel. Three apocalyptic destructions—the extinction of Indian civilization, the termination of Spanish colonialism and the Revolution itself—are only the landmarks in a story that has been a constant reworking of the themes of poverty, exploitation and frustrated aspirations. With such a past behind them, and with a future so threatening and uncertain—for all its hopeful signs—a mocking sense of humour may continue to stand the inhabitants of Mexico City in good stead. If it doesn't help them control their problematic city, it will help them to bear it—and even, perhaps, to go on loving it.

Aficionados of Spectacle and Sport

A crowd of spectators at a charreada ripples with varying reactions. The city has many specially built charro rings, where contests are held most weekends.

Because Mexicans so enjoy contest and spectacle they are enthusiastic followers of sports. Among their most popular games are two introduced from Spain. The lightning-fast competition called jai alai tests players' reflexes to the limit as opposing teams, using basket-like bats laced to their wrists, catch and fling a small, hard ball in a three-walled court. And, of course, there is bullfighting. Every Sunday during the seven-month professional season, crowds fill Mexico City's two rings (the 50,000-seat Plaza Mexico is the world's biggest) to witness the finely choreographed battles between matador and bull. Soccer and boxing are also followed keenly. But Mexico has a spectacle uniquely its own: the charreada, precursor of the rodeo. In these contests, amateur riders perform equestrian feats developed out of Mexico's rugged ranching traditions.

In traditional costume, a girl rider in a charreada puts her horse briskly through its paces.

Three charro contestants, in an event that exhibits both horsemanship and artistry with the lasso, work with intuitive co-ordination to catch an unbroken horse.

On the fringe of Mexico City, a dusty field and crudely drawn centre circle provide the essentials for neighbourhood players in a weekend soccer game.

The camera captures the balletic beauty of jai alai as a professional player practises solo. The painted numbers on the wall designate serving and receiving areas.

A referee leaps in to warn of an infraction of rules in a professional boxing bout at the Arena Coliseo, where matches are held four times a week.

Alone in the ring of the Plaza Mexico, under the knowledgeable gaze of a capacity crowd, a matador eludes the charging bull with a flourish of his cape.

Another matador—one of several to fight in a single afternoon—confronts the bull in a moment of stillness before delivering the final sword-thrust.

Unscathed from his encounter except for a torn and blood-stained costume, a triumphant matador is carried aloft to his waiting car by jubilant fans.

PIERCE OIL Co LONDON
STANDARD OIL Co N.Y.
TIERRA
LIBERTAD
Y PAN
PLAN DE Sn LUIS
1905
"REGENERACION"
REVOLUCION SOCIAL
1906-1907
1908

4

The Forging of a Nation

Every year, after nightfall on September 15, the Zócalo in Mexico City is thronged with thousands of people eagerly awaiting the ceremonial prelude to their greatest national fiesta. It is the eve of Independence Day, and all eyes are focused on the central balcony of the floodlit National Palace, above which hangs the *Campana de la Independencia*—the same church bell that Father Hidalgo rang in the town of Dolores to launch the 1810 rebellion against Spain. Here, at 11 p.m., the President of the Republic re-enacts that momentous event, tolling again Hidalgo's liberty bell and repeating the priest's celebrated *grito*, the rallying cry that first called the nation to rebellion: *"Viva Mexico! Viva la Independencia!"* Fireworks illuminate the night sky. Throughout the country, Mexicans begin celebrations commemorating their freedom from 300 years of Spanish rule.

The imposing National Palace, occupying the entire east side of the Zócalo, is the natural place for Mexico's annual outburst of patriotic rejoicing. It is, if you like, the most distinguished monument in a city that is full of statues, plaques and murals commemorating the epic progress of the Mexican people through the centuries of developing nationhood. Inside the National Palace all the leading players in the drama are depicted in one of Diego Rivera's most gigantic murals, a fresco—dazzling in its colour and detail—that sweeps over the monumental central staircase. In it one meets both the major figures—Cortés, Hidalgo, Maximilian, Juarez, Villa, Zapata and their peers—and a thousand lesser actors: bemedalled buffoons, sombreroed bandits, miserly capitalists, starving peasants, leering priests and evil-faced, corrupt judges.

Admittedly, the mural represents a Marxist view of Mexican history. Rivera was a socialist, like so many other leading artists of his day. He canonized the heroes of the 1910-20 Revolution, the peasants and the Aztec past and damned the representatives of capitalism, the Church and Spanish colonialism. He endowed some of his "good" characters with a more humanitarian motivation than they could honestly claim. But, his giant mural—painted between 1929 and 1935—is undeniably a masterpiece, one that sent me plunging into the history books and returning again and again to identify its vividly, often savagely, portrayed characters.

It is often said that modern Mexican history can be summed up in three words: Independence, Reform and Revolution. Of course that is an oversimplification; but by dividing the post-Hispanic years of political turmoil into three roughly equal periods—the first dating from the outbreak of Hidalgo's rebellion in 1810, the second from Juarez' great reforms in the

Grouped in this detail from a huge mural in the National Palace painted by Mexico's internationally celebrated Diego Rivera are key figures of the Revolution of 1910-20. Among those shown are two sword-wielding military dictators—Porfirio Díaz (extreme left) and Victoriano Huerta—and the early revolutionary leader Francisco Madero (right centre, wearing the presidential sash). In the background, foreign-owned oil rigs and a grand mansion symbolize the exploitation of the people.

1850s, and the third from the Revolution in 1910—one does get a helpful perspective on events, since one period may be said to have stored up conditions that created the next.

When it came in 1821, after 11 years of intermittent and bloody fighting, independence ushered in three decades of factional conflicts and national bankruptcy. The War of Independence had left the country in disarray. Many mines were closed and *haciendas* went untilled. Communications were appalling. Not a single rural road could be travelled without fear of bandits. Road surfaces, relatively well maintained during the colonial period, were fast deteriorating with neglect; and Mexico City had only one properly maintained link with the outside world: the steep, stony trail to Veracruz.

The ending of Spanish rule did nothing to remove the fundamental divisions in Mexican society. In fact, the Creole and mestizo classes that had combined to resist the Spaniards now started to compete with each other for control of the State. All the big landowners, bishops and senior army officers were Creoles. They were most influential in the capital and expected to inherit the privileges of the colonial establishment. They had little in common with the guerrilla freedom fighters and members of the liberal mestizo middle class—schoolmasters, minor civil servants, ranchers, small businessmen—who were mostly based in the provincial towns and had hoped, by expelling the Spanish, to establish a democratic republic. With the Spaniards gone, there were few men who had any experience of government or who showed themselves capable of establishing civil order and national unity. Heavy-handed generals with a taste for power and often a flair for double-dealing found it easy to establish themselves by military coups: between 1821 and 1850 there were more than 50 Mexican governments, some surviving only a few months, one for exactly 43 minutes.

Initially, one man stood out in the confusion, General Antonio López de Santa Anna, the supreme opportunist of 19th-Century Mexico. Crafty, charismatic, sometimes liberal, sometimes conservative, Santa Anna was surely the archetype of the Mexican military-political adventurer. Despite repeated disasters, both military and political, he constantly managed to reappear on the scene in the guise of national hero. During his 22 years in public life, he presided over 11 governments that spanned some of the most catastrophic years in Mexico's history.

In 1846, war broke out between Mexico and the United States over the issue of Texas. Though historically part of Mexico, Texas had declared its independence in 1836, and in 1845 it had been annexed by the American government and admitted as the 28th state of the Union. Mexico disputed the annexation. Santa Anna took command of the Mexican forces and, after fighting an inconclusive battle against General Zachary Taylor in the north, rushed south to intercept General Winfield Scott, who had landed

On top of the 150-foot-high column of the Monument of National Independence, a floodlit Winged Victory, known widely as "El Ángel", symbolizes the freedom from Spanish colonial rule that Mexico won by the protracted War of Independence of 1810-21. The statue, which was dedicated in 1910 for the independence centenary, was toppled by an earthquake in 1957. When it was re-installed, some Mexican wits therefore dubbed it "the fallen angel".

an army at Veracruz and was marching on Mexico City. By the summer of 1847, Santa Anna was directing a heroic defence of the doomed capital.

It was in Mexico City that the Americans encountered the sternest resistance, and they were greatly surprised. On provincial battlefields, Mexican forces had been largely composed of Indians; conscripted from *haciendas* and separated from their communities, lacking any great motivation to stand and fight, they deserted in large numbers. In Mexico City, by contrast, the defenders included many middle-class mestizos and students who had a true sense of patriotism and were prepared to die for their country. The last stronghold to fall was the castle on Chapultepec Hill, at that time housing a military academy. As American troops made their final assault on the morning of September 13, 1847, six of the cadets, some only 13 years old, wrapped themselves in the Mexican flag and leapt to immortality from the castle parapet. Today, at the entrance to Chapultepec Park, the boy martyrs are commemorated by the monument to Los Niños Héroes (The Boy Heroes): six colossal, eagle-topped columns ranged in a spectacular semicircle of marble.

The result of the war was catastrophic for Mexico. The government was forced to recognize the American annexation of Texas and to cede territory that encompassed the present-day states of Utah, Nevada and California, as well as New Mexico and Arizona north of the Gila River, plus parts of Colorado and Wyoming—an area larger than France and Germany combined. In his last dictatorship from 1853 to 1855, Santa Anna, in order to pay his troops, added to this appalling loss by selling to the United States a further 45,000 square miles: the southern parts of Arizona and New Mexico.

Hitherto, Mexico had been a factional society riven by class and caste distinctions—hardly a nation at all; and the ruinous war with the United States did little to heal the underlying divisions. But the shattering loss of so much territory did at least unite the Mexican people in their hatred of a common enemy. A new sense of nationalism was born that would play an important part in the revolutionary outbreaks of the next century.

In December, 1829, General Santa Anna had sat down to a dinner in the city of Oaxaca and was waited upon by a barefoot Zapotec Indian. Twenty-five years later, when the old general was deposed for the last time, that part-time waiter—an orphaned shepherd-boy, who was to become successively lawyer, judge and Governor of Oaxaca State—began to emerge as perhaps the most significant and certainly the most revered figure in Mexican history. His name was Benito Juarez.

In 1855, following the final overthrow of Santa Anna, Juarez came to Mexico City. There, as Minister of Justice in the country's first effective liberal government and later as President for a total of 14 years, he carried out a comprehensive programme of constitutional reforms—thereafter

Begun in the 18th Century as a viceregal residence, Chapultepec Castle has also served as an imperial palace and a presidential mansion. It is now a museum.

A school group pays homage at the Monument to the Boy Heroes—six cadets who, in 1847, died valiantly defending Chapultepec Castle against U.S. invaders.

known collectively as La Reforma. Juarez and his fellow ministers addressed themselves to the fundamental discontents that had been awaiting redress ever since the stillborn revolution of independence. Liberals had believed all along that a democratic, racially and socially equal society could never be created until the triple alliance of Church, army and great landowners was broken. Thus Juarez' measures abolished the special legal and tax privileges traditionally enjoyed by the clergy and the military. Church and State were separated, education was freed from clerical control, freedom of speech and of the Press were established.

The most important measures were those affecting the Church, which in colonial times had become the country's largest and wealthiest landowner, yet paid no taxes. Church estates were now confiscated and sold. The aims were to increase government revenue, stimulate the economy by putting the Church's enormous wealth into circulation, and to redistribute the Church's estates among the poor and landless Indian masses. But few peasants had the means to buy land and so the great sale of estates merely extended the rich landowning class: upper-class and middle-class Creoles for the most part, and also foreign investors.

The conservative establishment was outraged and the Church threatened to excommunicate any person who swore allegiance to the new constitution or who purchased expropriated Church lands. In 1858 a military revolt toppled the government and the army seized power. Juarez escaped to Veracruz, establishing a rival government there, and three years of civil war followed. Priests were shot for refusing to give Communion to liberal soldiers, churches and religious relics were wantonly destroyed and liberal sympathizers were executed by conservative generals.

At first the conservatives had the upper hand, but the tide turned and liberal armies closed in on Mexico City. In 1861 Juarez drove into the capital and assumed the presidency. By now the nation was at its lowest ebb since independence: suffering from lawlessness and bankruptcy, and owing vast debts to British, French and Spanish businessmen whose properties and interests had been damaged or confiscated during the civil war. Because the treasury was empty, Juarez decreed a two-year moratorium on all foreign debts. In retaliation, a joint European military force landed at Veracruz in 1862 to collect the outstanding debts. Juarez managed to come to an agreement with the Spanish and British, who withdrew; but the French under Napoleon III, nephew of the great Napoleon Bonaparte, had expansionary aims. They marched on Mexico City.

At Puebla, the one major city along the route from Veracruz, Mexico achieved its most famous victory. Four thousand Mexicans, fighting with obsolete weapons left over from the Battle of Waterloo and bought from the British, repelled 6,000 crack French troops. But there could be no ultimate victory. Napoleon sent in reinforcements 28,000-strong and, in the face of impossible odds, Juarez once again abandoned Mexico City.

On June 7, 1863, the French army marched into the undefended capital to be welcomed like liberators by Mexican conservatives and clergy, and even by ordinary people who hoped for an end to the banditry that had followed the civil war. Church bells rang and all the way to the Zócalo the French troops were bombarded with nosegays and garlands of flowers, and greeted with *vivas*. To swell the numbers, thousands of *peones* (labourers) were hired by conservative politicians to cheer the parading conquerors; their fee was three *centavos* a man, plus a liberal ration of liquor.

In August, 1863, Archduke Ferdinand Maximilian of Austria—the younger brother of the Emperor Franz Josef and a charming, liberal-minded, young dilettante—received a congratulatory telegram from Napoleon III. It informed Maximilian that, after a nation-wide plebiscite, the national assembly in Mexico City had proclaimed him Emperor of Mexico. Eight months later, deceived into believing that the Mexican people had voted overwhelmingly in his favour, Maximilian finally agreed to accept the throne and dedicate his life to the service of a country he had never seen.

From that moment the 31-year-old Archduke became the key pawn in a power game insidiously based on lies and deception. The conservative assembly that elected him Emperor was not remotely representative of the Mexican nation. Maximilian was being used—by Mexican conservatives and by the clergy who saw him (incorrectly, as it turned out) as a means for regaining the privileges and power threatened by Juarez' reforms; and also by Napoleon III, who dreamt unrealistically of emulating in Central America the successes his great namesake had achieved in Europe.

According to a treaty signed between Napoleon and Maximilian, France promised to maintain 20,000 supporting troops in Mexico until 1867; and for six years after that a Foreign Legion force of about 8,000 men. In exchange, the Emperor pledged to pay the expenses incurred by France in her activities on Mexican soil; and to settle all the claims lodged against Mexico by Spain, England and France in 1861. In order to pay off some claims at once, Maximilian was persuaded to take out a huge loan from French bankers—thus tripling the national debt overnight and condemning his new empire to long-term bankruptcy. Meanwhile, rattling over the northern countryside in his austere, black carriage, was the menacing figure of Benito Juarez, still considering himself the President and recognized as such by large sections of the population. As soon as the French military guarantee expired and troops were withdrawn, Juarez' return to power and the completion of his reforms were assured.

For me, there are no more tragic figures in Mexico's history than Maximilian and his ambitious wife, the Belgian Princess Charlotte. On June 12, 1864, their entry into Mexico City brought to the war-ravaged capital all the glittering pomp of European state ceremonial. Politics apart, the popular appeal of this glamorous young couple was undeniable. On

While occupying Mexico City briefly in 1914, the guerrilla Pancho Villa sits in the presidential chair with peasant leader Emiliano Zapata (right) at his side.

that day, when they were greeted with general rejoicing that enlivened the Zócalo until dawn, the smiling Maximilian and Carlota (already insisting on the Spanish version of her name) symbolized a new beginning and inspired a predominant feeling of hope: among the clergy, who confidently expected to see their property and rights restored; among the conservatives, who anticipated recovering privilege and power; among ordinary citizens, who longed for peace and stability. Yet, precisely three years and one week later, Maximilian would be dead from the bullets of a firing-squad and the beautiful Carlota would be confined to a castle in Italy and later in Belgium—a pathetic, demented figure destined to live on for 60 years in a world of fantasy and dark shadows, madly believing until the end that she was still Empress of Mexico.

So long afterwards, it is tempting to see this imperial adventure as tragic grand opera, with Maximilian and Carlota as Ruritanian characters creating in semi-feudal Mexico a totally irrelevant world of courtly elegance, refinement and splendour. The castle on Chapultepec Hill, built in the 18th Century as a viceregal residence and adopted by Maximilian as an escape from the barrack-like National Palace, bears witness to that brief and incongruous world of crystal-chandeliered magnificence. Here, amid ornate salons and marble halls that have been preserved as Maximilian and Carlota created them, one can readily visualize the state banquets with flunkeys serving the finest French cuisine, the lavish balls with crinolines swirling to Strauss waltzes. Here also, one can see the Emperor's ostentatious, Milan-made coach and—tellingly positioned alongside it, emphasizing the shallowness of Maximilian's position—the black carriage, so austere and battered, that served Juarez as his "presidential office" as he fled from town to town ahead of Napoleon's troops.

Maximilian was perhaps excessively extravagant in his embellishment of Chapultepec Castle and also self-indulgent in creating (as Cortés had done) a lavish country retreat amid the groves of oranges and mangoes in Cuernavaca, 40 miles away. Nevertheless, he was in many ways an enlightened and practical ruler. In four decades of independence, Mexico City had fallen steadily into decay. When Maximilian arrived, he found that many churches and monasteries, even the cathedral, urgently needed restoration. The streets, including those around the National Palace, were filthy and strewn with refuse. Squatting on sidewalks everywhere were so-called *leperos* or beggars—men, women and children permanently scarred by disease or disfigured in riots or wars. The Emperor resolved to rid the capital of so much squalor, and to a certain extent he succeeded.

He initiated many building projects, including—at Carlota's insistence —the laying down of the Paseo de la Reforma. He arranged for the central Alameda Park to be beautified with ornamental fountains, trees and flower beds. Similarly, he had the Zócalo redesigned as a delightful miniature park with fountains and benches and shady trees—an improvement

Skilled technicians, employed full-time to maintain Mexico City's many murals, go about restoring the vast design on one wall of the University of Mexico's central administration block. The mural, created by the distinguished artist David Alfaro Siqueiros in the 1950s, has a subject typical of the city's public works of art: scientists, humanists and artists symbolically offering their work for the benefit of the nation.

destroyed in 1956 when the plaza was laid bare and paved with concrete slabs to facilitate the staging of state ceremonies.

The imperial court and the sizeable new French population, both military and civilian, had a lasting influence on Mexican manners, fashion and music; and, artistically at least, French and Mexican traditions blended profitably. Maximilian and Carlota were vigorous patrons of the arts and the Emperor was primarily responsible for seeing that many pre-Columbian relics—now displayed in the National Museum of Anthropology—were rescued from jungles and warehouses and preserved.

The real tragedy of Maximilian's emperorship lies in the fact that he deserved a better fate. He genuinely loved Mexico and Mexicans; and, as a firm believer in liberal ideology, resisted the undemocratic demands of the conservatives and clergy who had brought him to Mexico. In open defiance of the papal nuncio, he upheld the nationalization of Church property and supported religious toleration.

Incurably romantic, naïvely idealistic, so often ill-advised by the arch-intriguers surrounding him, Maximilian was never less than honourable. Carlota's personal dislike of Mexico intensified in direct ratio to Maximilian's growing love of the country. Nevertheless, she stood firmly by her husband. And in the summer of 1866, when Napoleon threatened to withdraw his French troops from Mexico prematurely, it was Carlota who hastened to Europe to enlist support for the imperial cause against Juarez' republican forces, which were advancing on all fronts.

"I will be back in three months," Carlota promised. But she was never to see Mexico City again. After being rejected in Paris by Napoleon, she moved on to Italy to appeal to the Pope for support. There, bouts of irrationality that had marked her behaviour for months gave way to prolonged periods of total, sometimes violent, madness. During her audience with the Pope she became uncontrollably hysterical and soon after her insanity was confirmed by a leading specialist in nervous diseases.

News of Carlota's tragic fate persuaded Maximilian that there was nothing to be gained by abdicating and returning to Europe, and so he abandoned all thought of leaving Mexico. His decision amounted virtually to a death-wish. By February 1867, all French troops had been withdrawn. Yet Maximilian led his imperial army in a heroic last stand in the city of Querétaro, a hundred miles north of Mexico City. There, his garrison of 9,000 men held out for 72 days against republican forces at least four times more numerous. But the luckless Maximilian, already betrayed by Napoleon, was now betrayed by one of his own colonels, who opened the imperial defences to the enemy. Subsequently, in a farcical trial conducted on the stage of a local theatre, the Emperor of Mexico was condemned to death at a military tribunal by four votes to three.

There is a Mexican saying that goes: "Tell me how you die and I will tell you who you are." In dying, Maximilian showed himself to be a true son of his adopted Mexico. On the Cerro de las Campanas (Hill of the Bells) at Querétaro, on June 19, 1867, he gave each soldier in the seven-man firing-squad one ounce of gold and asked them to aim well for the body so that his mother could look once more upon his unmarked face. Finally he called out in Spanish: "I forgive everybody. I pray that everyone may also forgive me. And I pray that my blood, which is about to be shed, will flow for the good of the country. *Viva Mexico! Viva la Independencia!*"

In 1910, Mexico City was far and away the most impressive and colourful capital in Latin America. Its main streets were swept clean of dust and litter, and were empty of *leperos* and half-starved Indians; the flower beds of Alameda, Reforma and the Zócalo were in immaculate order; public buildings glistened in the sunlight with newly scrubbed freshness. It was the centenary year of Father Hidalgo's *grito de Dolores*, and dignitaries from all over the world were invited to attend month-long independence celebrations in September, to see how spectacularly Mexico had advanced into the 20th Century. This new Mexico was convincingly projected as a foreign investors' utopia: a country with stable government and industry, law and order, new railways, harbours, factories and drainage systems, and enormous mineral wealth that included newly discovered oil.

Such was the achievement claimed by Porfirio Díaz, the man who dominated Mexico for most of the 40-odd years after Maximilian's execution. Díaz, 80 years old in 1910, had been one of the republican generals in the war against Maximilian and the French. In 1876, four years after President Juarez died of a heart attack soon after being elected for his fourth term of office, Díaz had seized power and soon emerged as the most effective despot Latin America has ever known. Like Juarez, he was a man of humble origins from Oaxaca. Unlike Juarez, he was prepared to sacrifice democratic and liberal principles for the sake of preserving power and furthering his dominant goals: the economic development and diplomatic independence of his country.

In one sense his achievement was genuine. During the three decades of his regime—the so-called Porfiriato—foreign trade multiplied tenfold. Internal trade was revolutionized by the laying of some 12,000 miles of railway track. The value of mining products more than trebled. U.S. investment rose to more than a billion dollars. And in 1894 Díaz' brilliant finance minister, José Yves Limantour, had presented the first balanced budget in Mexican history. In 1910, national income stood at $1,000 million and there was actually a budgetary surplus of $136 million.

But there was another side to Díaz' glowing picture of national well-being. Mexico City's main streets were indeed empty of beggars—but only because they had been ordered to keep out of sight. Similarly, the countryside was free of widespread banditry only because the President had put the bandits in uniform, creating a corrupt and trigger-happy rural

On October 2, 1968, ten days before the opening of the Olympic Games, a student rally in the Plaza of the Three Cultures ended in tragedy as the Mexican government sent in armed riot police supported by armoured cars and tanks. An estimated 200 people were killed and several thousand injured or arrested as a result of official reaction to student demands for political reforms.

police force called the *rurales*. There was a minimum of industrial strife only because organized strikes were swiftly ended by military force and a minimum of political unrest only because dangerous opponents of the government were promptly jailed or exiled.

Society had remained strangely static. Although the power of the Church had been permanently broken by the reforms of Juarez, the army remained as powerful as ever under Díaz' control; and the landowning class had become, if anything, more powerful. After the sale of Church lands, more than half the nation's territory had ended up in the hands of less than 30,000 families. *Haciendas* were so enormous (one in Chihuahua encompassed seven million acres) that in many cases they functioned like independent kingdoms, with towns and villages under the landowner's absolute control. Foreign investors, lured by lavish tax concessions and gifts of land, had acquired a disproportionate influence over the economy. The newly developed industries were largely foreign-controlled, chiefly by Americans; and Spaniards and Cubans owned most of the cultivated land, thus perpetuating colonial conditions long after independence.

The liberal mestizo middle class found new prosperity acting as lawyers and providing other professional services for foreign companies, but felt more and more like second-class citizens. The vast mass of Indian peasants had so far remained outside the struggle between the upper echelons of society, but their social and economic conditions were appalling. The expropriation of the Indian *ejidos* or communal lands, begun in colonial times and continued ever since, proceeded with a new ruthlessness.

Those who rebelled were either slaughtered or sold into slavery on plantations and in mines. By 1910, nine million of the 10 million people employed in agriculture—very nearly two-thirds of the total population—were landless. Working as *peones* on the vast *haciendas*, they lived a life of medieval serfdom. The white *hacendados* ruled like feudal lords, exercising power over mayors, judges, priests and police alike. So little did they consider their *peones'* interests that, during the Porfiriato, per capita production of maize and beans—the two staples in the Indian diet—dwindled by half and three-quarters respectively. Meanwhile, the *peones* toiled to produce cash crops such as sugar and wheat, and the country had to import foodstuffs for the first time in its history. To make matters worse, real wages, already a pittance, declined by nearly 25 per cent between 1898 and 1910. By the time Díaz was ready to stage his celebrations for the centenary of independence, a large part of the Mexican population was on the verge of starvation. Only a new leader with a new *grito* was needed, and the whole of Mexico would erupt in a paroxysmal conflict.

In April of that fateful year 1910, a strange ball of fire streaked through the sky, night after night. Mexican newspapers explained that it was Halley's comet; but many citizens, illiterate and deeply superstitious, interpreted it as a portent of death and destruction. That same month, the old dictator Díaz, now seeking re-election for the sixth consecutive term, had his first warning of political trouble. In Mexico City's Tivoli Theatre, the newly formed Anti-Re-Electionist Party proclaimed Francisco Madero, an idealistic intellectual, as its rival presidential candidate. The party's cardinal aim was to prevent the rise of further dictators by prohibiting any Mexican from serving more than one term as President. All over the country, clubs were formed to support Madero's candidacy.

Díaz left nothing to chance; he had Madero arrested and, in June, emerged triumphant from a rigged election. Once the centenary celebrations in September were safely over, Madero was released on bail. He fled to San Antonio, Texas, and from that safe distance he declared the Mexican elections null and void. At the same time—under pressure from militant supporters—he proclaimed himself the provisional President of the Republic and called on the Mexican people to rise up against the Díaz regime, naming November 20 as the date for the Revolution to begin.

Madero was the most improbable of revolutionary leaders: a wealthy, high-born *hacendado* who, as a student in Paris, had been converted to spiritualism and had become deeply impressed with the democratic way of life. He had the noblest of motives, but neither the ruthlessness nor the political cunning necessary to hold together the factional forces he inspired. On November 19, he crossed the frontier into Mexico with a small group of supporters. But Díaz had acted first and arrested many of the revolutionary leaders. Madero could find only 25 men armed and ready to fight. Discouraged, he fled to New Orleans and was waiting there for a ship to Europe when he learnt that the Revolution had started

The Chamber of Deputies, the lower house of Mexico's Congress, occupies a sumptuous hall built in 1910 during the dictatorship of President Porfirio Díaz. On the far wall rolls of honour, added after construction, record in gold lettering the names of heroes of the War of Independence—and of the Revolution that finally toppled Díaz from power in 1911.

without him. As soon as he believed the insurgents had a chance of success, he returned to Mexico to join them.

For the first time the rural masses had become politically active. In the northern state of Chihuahua, a storekeeper, Pascual Orozco, and a cattle rustler, Doroteo Arango (later calling himself Pancho Villa), had organized guerrilla bands and successfully attacked federal troops on November 27. Soon afterwards, in the state of Morelos, directly south of Mexico City, another peasant army gathered under a tenant farmer who became one of the chief champions of the rural poor in their demands for land re-distribution, Emiliano Zapata. Zapata's forces stormed the city of Cuerna-vaca, and within a few months, guerrilla bands were operating nation-wide —burning *haciendas*, raiding trains and banks, ambushing federal troops, and riding into battle to shouts of the new *grito*: "Land and Liberty!" Within six months, the aged Díaz had fled to Paris. In 1911, Madero called for elections and gained the presidency almost without opposition.

Yet this was still only the beginning of the most confused of all modern revolutions, a social upheaval that lasted for 10 years. It was in reality a civil war, in which the newly aroused peasant masses and the long-frustrated middle-class reformists fought the conservatives and each other for control of the State. It produced so many leaders that Mexicans called them *generales de dedo* ("finger generals"), because you had to count them off on your fingers to remember who they all were. In February, 1913, President Madero was treacherously ousted and put to death by General Victoriano Huerta, who made himself President and established a new reign of terror in the Díaz style. The subsequent struggle to over-throw Huerta united the revolutionary forces, but it also gave opportunities to more conservative-minded leaders, most notably Venustiano Carranza, the white-bearded Governor of the northern state of Coahuila. Carranza took charge of the revolt in the north, declared himself First Chief of the Constitutionalist Army and astutely allied himself to General Álvaro Obregón, a politically shrewd rancher from the state of Sonora.

Obregón commanded a powerful army composed largely of fierce Yaqui Indians. By August 1914, the revolutionary armies were marching on Mexico City, and Obregón won the race, arriving ahead of the advancing armies of Villa and Zapata. Huerta escaped to the United States, but the victors could not agree on who should emerge as President. Thereafter, almost all the leading figures of the Revolution fought against each other at some time or another: Villa against Carranza, Obregón against Villa, Carranza against Obregón, Carranza against General Plutarco Elías Calles, an ex-schoolteacher. And, ultimately, almost all of them met with violent deaths. Although much of the fighting was done far from Mexico City, possession of the capital was a powerful claim to political legitimacy. During the course of the Revolution, Mexico City was occupied five times by various armies and the modernized city of the Porfiriato was reduced by degrees to a shambles.

One truly important achievement of the Revolution was the drafting of the 1917 constitution. Out of the quarrels of 1914 and 1915, Carranza had emerged supreme. In 1916 he called a convention to draft a new constitution on traditional liberal lines. A year later the document was ready. Although Carranza had packed the convention with moderate supporters, the more radical members carried the day. It reaffirmed the 19th-Century reform laws regarding public education and the restricted position of the Catholic Church. It condemned the *hacienda* system, called for a return of the land to the people, declared all subsoil resources to be the property of the republic, recognized the right of workers to strike, to engage in collective bargaining, to receive equal pay, sickness benefits and pensions. Carranza never came to terms with these sweeping provisions, particularly the agrarian reforms: during his presidency, he distributed to the peasants a mere 450,000 acres—barely one large *hacienda*. But the constitution remained on the statute books, ready to be enforced by later governments with the political opportunity and the will to do so.

In 1920, elections were due. However, Carranza had no wish to give up power, and so once again a revolutionary force marched on Mexico City, this time under General Calles. Carranza took flight to Veracruz on a special train loaded with federal funds and treasure, but he was intercepted, hunted down in the mountains and murdered in his sleep. In the ensuing election the victor was Carranza's old colleague, General Álvaro Obregón. He was the first of the 11 Presidents since Díaz to survive a full four-year term. His election marked the end of one of the most significant decades in Mexico's political history, a decade also of indescribable

In Mexico City's burgeoning Stock Exchange, founded in 1894, brokers trade beneath a gallery where officials record the prices of deals already concluded.

savagery and horror. By its end, a million Mexicans—6 per cent of the total population—had been killed or had died of epidemics and starvation.

To my mind, the most telling reminder in Mexico City today of those savage times is to be seen within a rectilinear, two-storey monument of concrete and marble that stands in a small, attractive plaza off Insurgentes. Here, in an illuminated recess, is a relic to match the nightmarish quality of the revolutionary struggle for land and liberty. It is the right hand and wrist of Álvaro Obregón, pickled in a jar and permanently kept on public display. It is a grotesque sight: the hand a sickly shade of white and the nerves and ganglia drifting beneath it. The tortured fist is half clenched as though reaching out, like the divided leaders of the Revolution, for something that could never be completely grasped.

In 1915, during a battle in which Villa was decisively defeated, a grenade had exploded beside Obregón, shattering his right arm. His agony was so unbearable that he drew his service pistol, put it to his head, and pulled the trigger. There was only a dull, metallic click. One of Obregón's captains had cleaned the pistol the previous day and, by a thousand-to-one chance, had forgotten to reload it. Obregón's arm was amputated and the chosen part preserved.

The Obregón Monument stands on the former site of a restaurant where, in 1928, the general was assassinated. The killer, who was arrested and later executed, was a fervent Catholic, and so the murder was attributed, inconclusively, to extremists seeking the restoration of Church power. Whatever the motive, Obregón was a natural target for extremists. Three weeks before, he had become the first President since Díaz to be elected to a second term, contrary to the fundamental principle of no re-election established by Madero. He and the previous President, Calles, had persuaded Congress to concede that the no re-election principle applied to a President seeking a second *successive* term, and to extend the presidential term, formerly four years, to six years. By these means the two men sought to share power between themselves: but they also genuinely believed that re-elections were necessary to establish governmental continuity and to see policies through to their proper conclusion. When Obregón was killed and the presidency left open to anyone, including political opponents, Calles needed another means of perpetuating his policies. His solution was to organize a new political party.

Since its formation in 1929, the official revolutionary party, now called the Partido Revolucionario Institucional (PRI), has continuously held the presidency and all the governorships of the federated states that make up the republic, and the great majority of the seats in both the upper and lower chambers of Congress. The party works by ensuring advancement for loyal and co-operative aspirants to influence and wealth, and closing any other real route to power. It allocates seats to all the important

A citizen expounds his views from a "free speech" platform facing a statue of Beethoven in Alameda Park. Placards on the left state conditions under which the platform may be used for constructive criticism: citizens must speak for no more than five minutes, refrain from insults and slander, not make use of prepared documents; the government may take notes and may also demand the name and address of every speaker.

interests and pressure groups that fought so bitterly during the Revolution: organized labour, peasants, and a large and heterogeneous grouping called the Popular Sector, including civil servants, the military, the liberal professions and small businessmen.

Legal opposition parties exist, both to the left and to the right of the PRI; indeed, they are encouraged as a controlled channel for the expression of dissent by a law that guarantees them a minimum number of seats in Congress. But the largest of these parties—the right-wing National Action Party (PAN)—has never achieved more than 12 per cent of any electoral vote, and the others are far behind.

Power is delegated downwards from the all-powerful political apex— the presidency—not mandated upwards from the electorate. Loyalty and support are secured by favours to people whose help will be useful. Even trade union membership is a privilege to be bought, inherited or earned by loyal service. This system of patronage can be unscrupulously exploited for personal gain, and it often is; but it would be glib to dismiss it merely as corrupt. In a country that has seen revolution so recently and still has deep social divisions, it offers the important gain of political stability.

When in 1968, discontent with the government of President Gustavo Díaz Ordaz aroused big student demonstrations in Mexico City, shortly before the Olympic Games, the government called out the army and a large number of students (estimated at more than 200) were killed at the Plaza of the Three Cultures. But afterwards, dissident leaders who were about to graduate received offers of good jobs in the administration. Since well-paid jobs are still scarce and fiercely sought after in Mexico, some of the young dissidents were glad to accept. By this process, the government disarmed potential enemies and at the same time gained able friends.

In Mexico City today, when the conversation turns to social problems, people often say with a wry smile: "Ah yes, if Benito Juarez were alive today, he'd die." Mexicans are very fond of using ironical phrases as a shield against unpleasant realities and I have heard this remark countless times. But would Juarez, I wonder, really be so disappointed by the social and economic progress that has taken place since his day?

There are still a few people who can remember the grim days before the Revolution. Hearing them recount their memories, it is not difficult to recognize that, for all its problems, Mexico is now measurably a better place in which to live than it was then. A Mexican peasant born in 1900 could expect to live only 27 years; today the average life expectancy is more than twice as long. The literacy rate, probably not higher than 15 per cent in 1916, has risen to more than 75 per cent; infant mortality has fallen from close on 40 per cent in some areas to 6 per cent.

One Sunday morning, a few years ago, I got into conversation with an elderly, smartly dressed stranger who was sitting next to me on a low wall beside a lake in Chapultepec Park. Señor Soto Rodriguez, then 70, was still active as a skilled carpenter. He told me how his father had been killed while fighting under Villa. "I was six years old when he died. But I can still remember those days—the *zócalo* in Puebla, and how one federal captain lined up 40 civilians in the square and had them shot because they supported Villa. In those days in Puebla, the military had you shot if they heard you voice one word of sympathy for Villa."

Señor Rodriguez had received only a primary education and that was frequently interrupted by revolutionary upheavals that closed down the school. By contrast, his four children had gained advanced education: two were in civil administration, one was a psychiatrist and one a chemist. "Of course, life is much better now," he said. "We live in a way my father never knew." Even so, he was soon expressing universal middle-class grievances: inflation was terrible, and it was difficult to make ends meet.

I have met several other survivors of the revolutionary period, but the most unusual was a wiry old gentleman whom I first saw when I was visiting the revolving restaurant at the top of the 52-storey Hotel de Mexico. He wore an old trilby hat, dusty shoes and a crumpled suit, and seemed completely out of place in the luxurious surroundings. It turned out that he was Manuel Suarez, a multimillionaire hotel magnate, and he was inspecting the progress of work on the still unfinished hotel.

Later, in a rare interview, the eccentric Señor Suarez talked to me about his astonishing career. He had been a stall-attendant in Mexico City's main market, La Merced, when the Revolution began. At 18, he ran off to join Villa's army and promptly gained the rank of lieutenant-colonel. Under Villa, as an officer in charge of army supplies, he gained valuable administrative experience. After the Revolution he established a cement factory with President Obregón's sponsorship. In the 1930s he bought his first hotel, the Casino de la Selva in Cuernavaca, soon to become famous as the setting of Malcolm Lowry's classic novel *Under the Volcano*. Now, at 82, he was still planning projects, working a full week and presiding over a family of 20 children and 60 grandchildren and great-grandchildren.

Considering his revolutionary past and his spectacular business success, Señor Suarez struck me as a perfect symbol of the change that has come over the Revolution. Before the uprising, economic and political power was in the hands of the tiny Creole minority, successors of the Spanish colonial rulers. When the Revolution began, peasants and workers gave a strong thrust to anti-capitalism. But in the hands of the middle-class generals who soon took over its leadership, the greatest upheaval in Mexico's history laid the foundations, not for an egalitarian commonwealth, but for a new plutocracy. Today, powerful élites are once more established in Mexico City; and though the revolutionary State clothes its actions with radical rhetoric, it remains true to the spirit of the capital's history—largely divorced from the needs of the masses.

Ten Tragic Days

Under the eyes of bystanders, National Palace Guards, loyal to the government of the ill-fated President Madero, await the enemy's advance on February 9, 1913.

In 1913, Mexico City was the setting for one of the Mexican Revolution's bloodiest dramas, known as the Tragic Ten Days. Six months after the Revolution began in 1910, the old dictator Porfirio Díaz had been ousted from the presidency he had held for 35 years by a liberal democrat, Francisco Madero. But on Sunday, February 9, 1913, reactionaries attempted a coup by attacking the National Palace in the Zócalo. The attempt failed, but President Madero entrusted the task of mopping up opposition to generals who were secretly in league with the insurrectionists. After 10 days of Machiavellian scheming, and artillery bombardments, the conspirators captured Madero; a few days later he was dead. By then thousands had been killed in the city, and Mexico's struggle for democracy was ended, for the time being, by the establishment of a new dictatorship.

After the attack, Sunday-morning sightseers crowd into the Zócalo past the cathedral and grant the coup's first victims the scant tribute of a passing glance.

Surrounded by supporters, President Madero arrives on horseback from his official residence to assess the outcome of the attack on the National Palace. Acting with uncharacteristic decisiveness, Madero sentenced the captured reactionary leaders to death. He regarded the opposition as virtually annihilated.

First Blood

The first of the Tragic Ten Days set a sickening pattern of casual slaughter. At 7 a.m. on February 9, the insurrectionist General Bernardo Reyes with 200 cavalry advanced on the National Palace, assuming that plans to win over the Palace Guard had succeeded. In fact, the Guard still supported Madero and opened fire, killing not only Reyes and many of his men, but also 200 innocent civilians on their way to mass at the cathedral adjacent to the palace. A second insurrectionist detachment, led by Felix Díaz (nephew of the former dictator) and Manuel Mondragón, was on its way to the Zócalo to join Reyes; but at the sound of firing they turned back in alarm and instead occupied the Ciudadela, the city's main arsenal and barracks a mile and a half away. It seemed only a matter of time before they would be dislodged.

Conspiracy and Nightmare

After his first success, President Madero made a suicidal decision: he replaced his Commander-in-Chief, Lauro Villar, who had been wounded, with General Victoriano Huerta, despite suspicions that Huerta was treacherous. He put another trustworthy man, General Aureliano Blanquet, in command of the palace garrison.

Huerta's orders were to bombard the Ciudadela and drive out Díaz and Mondragón. But Huerta had been conspiring with the enemy all along. To produce the illusion of real conflict, he and Díaz shelled the city from their respective positions. The result was both farcical and tragic. The Ciudadela was hit only once during a week's wild firing but city life turned into a nightmare. Corpses piled up in the streets, water and electricity were cut off, food became scarce.

The American Ambassador, Henry Lane Wilson, keen to see an end to the carnage and convinced that a take-over by Díaz would best serve American business interests, pressed for Madero's resignation; but Madero, still blindly trusting in Huerta to finish off the conspirators, would not comply.

Boldly flagging its neutrality, an American Embassy car takes Ambassador Henry Lane Wilson on a round of negotiations designed to put an end to the bloodshed and ease the conservative Felix Díaz into the presidency.

Safe inside the Ciudadela, Díaz (right) and Mondragón amuse themselves with calculations for a bombardment of the National Palace. No attack was seriously contemplated, nor was it necessary; General Blanquet—like Huerta, secretly on the side of the insurrectionists— was ready to open the gates whenever required.

Under General Huerta's command, government forces move towards the Ciudadela. During one such attack, seeing an opportunity to destroy troops who were loyal to Madero, the turncoat Huerta deliberately sent them on a frontal attack across an open square, where enemy machine-gunners simply mowed them down.

Laden with possessions, panic-stricken families take advantage of a 24-hour cease-fire on February 16 to escape from an area suffering heavy bombardment.

A Rigged Election

On February 18, the conspirators delivered the *coup de grâce*. General Blanquet, in command of the National Palace, arrested Madero at gunpoint. Huerta, Díaz and Ambassador Lane Wilson met at the American Embassy to decide on Madero's successor and agreed that Huerta should be installed as interim President, pending elections which would be rigged in favour of Díaz. A few days later, Madero and his Vice-President, Pino Suárez, were shot.

But surprisingly, when presidential elections were held on October 26, 1913, Huerta —who was not even a candidate—emerged with a majority and Díaz promptly fled the country. Just nine months later, however, in July 1914, Huerta was himself driven from Mexico by a former supporter, Venustiano Carranza, and the violence and treachery that had marked the Tragic Ten Days started all over again. It continued to disturb Mexico with unnerving regularity for another six years.

The National Palace courtyard (above) swarms with insurrectionists shortly after the coup on February 18. At the time, the newly arrested Madero and most of his Cabinet were being held under guard in the presidential suite.

President Huerta (centre) drives to the Chamber of Deputies accompanied by Vice-President Blanquet (left), and the Foreign Secretary, Querido Moheno.

5

A Full-Blooded Faith

One March afternoon a few years ago, I was standing in a vast crowd on the lower slopes of the Cerro de la Estrella (Hill of the Star) in Ixtapalapa, once an Aztec town and now a south-eastern district of Mexico City. Below us, to the north and the west, lay the interminable sprawl of the world's largest city. Yet the megalopolis was invisible beneath gathering storm clouds. At the base of the hill, where more onlookers were massed by the roadside, a long-bearded, red-cloaked man was swinging by the neck from a solitary tree, his tortured face hideously lit by the intermittent flicker of forked lightning, his tongue hanging grotesquely from his gaping mouth. Not far beyond, another man—barefoot, stripped to the waist and carrying a giant wooden cross—had fallen down on blood-stained knees and was grovelling in the dust while two Mexicans in the uniforms of Roman centurions lashed him with leather whips.

It was Good Friday, and we were waiting for the climax of the Ixtapalapa Passion Play, performed every year by a committee of residents and universally acknowledged to be the most spectacular in Mexico City. Of course we knew that Judas Iscariot, swinging so realistically from the tree, was well supported by a hidden harness and that his bloated tongue was an artful prop. But much else was real, including the blood on the scratched knees of Christ and the occasional whiplash that actually connected with his bare back. As we waited, the promised storm finally broke, unleashing gale-force winds that whirled blinding, choking dust into our mouths, nostrils and eyes. Torrential rain followed, and in a few minutes the temperature plunged by perhaps 20°F. We were drenched and chilled to the bone.

"Don't move away," a voice boomed over the loudspeaker system. "Never mind the weather. It is a sign. You are supposed to suffer on this day. After all, there was a hurricane, and thunder and lightning when Jesus was really crucified."

Only a few hours before, we had been sweltering in the narrow streets of the Ixtapalapa town centre while we watched local citizens enacting the arrest and trial of Jesus. Now it was 4.30 in the afternoon. Struggling up the hillside through the wind and rain came two columns of purple-robed volunteer penitents called Nazarenes: 260 young men of Ixtapalapa, mostly in their teens, each wearing a crown of sharp-pointed thorns, each dragging from his right shoulder a black cross that varied in height from five to eight feet and in weight from 100 to 150 pounds, according to how much he chose to punish himself. For more than two hours the Nazarenes

Amid a thunderstorm, amateur actors recreate the Crucifixion—the climax of the annual Passion Play held in Ixtapalapa, a south-eastern suburb of Mexico City. The angel precariously poised above Jesus represents a consoling envoy sent by God. In the background, a red-cloaked actor playing a Roman soldier (partly obscured) helps to steady the cross.

had been shuffling barefoot over sun-baked cobbles; now some were in acute distress and needed a helping hand. Between their two columns, I could see the agonized figure of the man playing Christ, staggering under the weight of his huge cross. As he turned off the road to begin the hill climb, he paused. "Keep moving!" shouted one of the centurions, cracking his whip. Jesus of Ixtapalapa stumbled on, falling so heavily once that he was briefly trapped beneath the cross.

I knew that not all I was witnessing was acting. Only a few days earlier I had visited this man, an 18-year-old taxi-driver named Carlos Rivas, at his parents' home. Carlos invited me to lift his cross, which he had bought with his own savings for 1,200 pesos. Made of solid pine, it was eight feet high and weighed 165 pounds. I could shift it no more than a couple of yards. But after almost a year of training Carlos could now move it nearly three miles, in face of very real intimidation by the men in breastplates and plumed helmets; they clearly relished their villainous roles and wielded their swords and whips with alarming vigour. In addition to the blood on his knees, Carlos had blisters on his feet, weals on his back and scratches on his head from the needle-like thorns of his crown.

The re-enactment of the Crucifixion coincided neatly with the worst of the tempest. Carlos, attached by metal rings with simulated nails and lashed by icy rain, remained on the cross for 15 minutes while Romans and the two condemned robbers on crosses to either side of him spoke their scripted lines. Then, half frozen, he was taken down, draped in a shroud, and borne down the hillside by six "disciples" before being spirited away to receive pain-killing injections and a medical check-up. It would be several weeks before he recovered completely.

Every Good Friday, all over Mexico, there are realistic reconstructions of the Crucifixion. None, however, has a more significant setting than the Passion Play on the Cerro de la Estrella. It was on this same hill that the Aztecs of Tenochtitlan assembled at the end of every sacred cycle of 52 years to await either the end of the world or the beginning of a new cycle. Since the Aztec calendar did not exactly accord with the annual cycle of the sun, every 52 years there was a five-day period of adjustment marked by fasting and penitence and by the extinction of all flames. It ended at midnight with a "new fire" ritual; it was held that the earth would remain in darkness for ever if the priests were unable to rekindle fire.

In their *teocalli* on the top of this same hill, the priests sought to avert the apocalypse by opening the chest of a sacrificial victim with an obsidian knife, tearing out the palpitating heart and kindling fire in the gaping cavity. This they did by twirling a tinder-dry stick against a small board of wood until it smouldered. Flames were coaxed up and then a great bonfire, built on the corpse, signalled far and wide that the world was saved for another half century. The "new fire" ceremony was last performed in 1507, 12 years before the conquistadors marched into the valley to subjugate

Congregants assemble for a mass in the modern Basilica of Guadalupe (left), consecrated in 1976 to house Latin America's most revered religious relic: a dark-skinned portrait of the Virgin of Guadalupe, holy patroness of Mexico. The painting—the only image in the basilica—hangs in a gilded frame behind the high altar. Visitors seeking a closer look at the image pass directly below it on a travellator (above).

and plunder the empire of Moctezuma II, destroy all temples and idols, and impose on all Indian peoples the "true religion"—Catholicism.

The Ixtapalapa Passion Play has grown enormously in popularity since it was first held in 1743 and, according to some reports, it now attracts crowds of half a million every year. In a country where anticlericalism is long established and even enshrined in the constitution, it may seem perplexing that the many festivals that fill the Mexican calendar should be occasions for such massive demonstrations of religious feeling. But the bitter rivalry between the Church and the government (whether liberal or revolutionary) has often gone over the heads of the Indian and mestizo people, leaving them to develop their own local forms of Catholicism.

Mexico holds about one-twelfth of the world's 724 million Catholics, but this fact obscures wide differences in religious practice. Among the upper and middle classes religious observance is orthodox, although—as in most great Western cities—it has been eroded by materialism. At the start of the three-day national holiday in Holy Week, the roads out of Mexico City are jammed with tens of thousands of cars heading for camping areas, for the nearest beaches and for the flesh-pots of Acapulco. The hundreds of thousands of people who go instead to Ixtapalapa include many from the humbler levels of society, whose faith has evolved out of a syncretism of Christian tenets and pagan beliefs, the origins of which go back to the earliest days of Spanish colonialism.

Many of the friars who followed in the wake of the conquistadors were inspired by a genuinely altruistic desire to bring Christianity to the inhabitants of Mexico, as well as to protect them from the cruelty and exploitation of the newly arrived colonists. In attempting to convert the Indians, the friars struck compromises, taking advantage of any similarities they could find between the Aztec and Catholic observances—explaining, for instance, the symbolic sacrifice of Christ by reference to the Aztecs' own concept of sacrifice. Both religions also involved the practices of penance and fasting, and had analogous ceremonies, such as baptism and marriage.

The Indians were allowed to preserve their ritual songs and dances, though these were re-dedicated to God. Jesus was seen as a reincarnation of Quetzalcoatl, and Catholic saints as equivalents of the many Aztec gods of lesser status. Dread of perpetual darkness was re-expressed as fear of eternal damnation. The fact that the friars wore habits that happened to resemble the black, hooded robes of the Aztec priests pre-disposed the Indians to accept their authority in religious matters. Such parallels greatly assisted the process of mass conversion, which in many areas went forward at a startling rate. One Franciscan was said to have baptized more than 200,000 Indians within a decade of Cortés' arrival, on occasion as many as 14,000 in one ceremony.

The intelligent and compassionate friars who followed Cortés were gradually superseded by priests who often showed little interest in the

Elements of three distinct eras of Mexican history meet at the Plaza of the Three Cultures, an extensive government project completed in 1965. In the foreground stand the excavated remains of the Aztecs' Great Pyramid of Tlatelolco; beyond the pyramid loom the spires of the 16th-Century Church of Santiago, built by the Spanish with stone taken from the ancient temple; in the background rise the concrete tiers of the offices and apartment blocks created by the modern, secular State.

people and made it clear that their first duty was to serve the spiritual needs of the rich Spanish overlords. From this well-gauged alliance the Church gained its huge endowments of land and property, gold and silver. Throughout colonial times, all the higher clergy in the cities and towns were Spanish-born, loyal to the Crown, largely immune from civil law, and rigidly opposed to any heretical ideas, such as the principle of social equality, that implied a challenge to the Church's authority. When the struggle for independence began, they reaped much of the resentment that the Creoles and mestizos felt towards the Spanish ruling élite.

Out in the rural areas, among the Indians and the lower ranks of the clergy, things were rather different. The Indians had accepted the outward forms of Catholicism—the churches, saints' images, processions and rituals—but they had not wholly abandoned their old beliefs. As late as the 19th Century, travellers in rural Mexico brought back tales of Aztec figurines placed beneath the sculpted images of Christian saints, in an effort to keep alive the spirit of the ancient religion. The provincial clergy, mostly Creole or mestizo by birth, were often much closer to the local population than to the upper ranks of the Church hierarchy, from which they were strictly excluded. They also had their ears open to the democratic and liberal ideas popularized by the French Revolution and the American War of Independence; and from the ranks of the lower clergy came some of the early leaders of the independence movement, including the Creole Hidalgo and his successor, the mestizo Morelos.

After Mexico gained its independence in 1821, control of the central Church hierarchy passed from Europeans to the Mexican-bred clergy; and characteristically Mexican forms of folk Catholicism began to develop, particularly in remote areas where the Indian peasants might receive visits from a priest no more than once or twice a year. The Church's central establishment, though weakened by the reforms of the mid-19th Century and by internal disputes, regained much of its past strength under the Díaz dictatorship and once more became closely identified with the ruling élite. In some areas during this period, the lower clergy were often called upon to mediate between landlords and protesting peasants; and, although continuing to espouse the interests of the rural population, they too sometimes came to be associated by the mass of the people with an oppressive establishment. Thus, when the Revolution broke in 1910, the Church was one of the principal losers.

During the 1920s the strict enforcement of the anticlerical clauses in the 1917 constitution—those limiting the number of priests permitted to work in each state, and prohibiting priests and nuns from teaching in primary schools or taking any part in politics—led to a backlash in the intensely Catholic states of the north and west that broke out into open civil war in 1926. Large numbers of the landed peasantry and the provincial townspeople formed guerrilla groups calling themselves the *cristeros*

Ornate, gilded columns studded with polychrome statuary adorn the Altar of the Kings in the Metropolitan Cathedral. Built between 1718 and 1737 by archit

ronimo de Balbas and gilded in 1743, the altar is Mexico City's earliest example of the Churrigueresque: an opulent baroque style imported from Spain.

(defenders of Christ). They attacked army garrisons, pillaged and burnt government buildings, and once even dynamited a train, killing a hundred passengers. The revolt provoked savage reprisals from government troops, who shot many priests and looted insurgent villages. Hostilities petered out in 1929, but the Church had been severely shaken by the conflict and remained at a low ebb all through the Thirties.

When the English Catholic novelist Graham Greene visited Mexico in 1938 to write his study of the Church under persecution, *The Lawless Roads*, he found that there were only 500 priests in the country still carrying out their pastoral duties. Mass was often celebrated in secret.

The anticlerical statutes in Mexico's constitution still stand, but they are widely ignored. The State now welcomes the help given to the country's education by Church schools and universities. Some priests are once again on the left in politics, speaking out on behalf of the poor and oppressed, and incurring the disapproval of their superiors and even the government for their popular stance. But what seems to me most significant is not the differences between radical and conservative clergy or between Church and State, but the fact that priests have played a comparatively unimportant part in the daily religious life of a large proportion of the Mexican population. As a result, religious life for the majority of Mexicans has always been largely a matter of direct approaches to their own saints and miraculous images.

In Mexico City I have often seen people kneeling at the altar steps with their eyes fixed on a painting of the Virgin Mary, talking to her as naturally and openly as if they were consulting a revered family friend. Some churches provide boxes where people may deposit letters asking favours of their local patron saints, who are expected to solve all kinds of problems—from stilling earthquakes to making barren women fertile. Some saints are deemed more efficient than others and become famous for their miraculous powers. Single girls looking for a husband are advised to collect 13 centavos and on St. Anthony's Day to donate the money to the saint. So literal is the faith of some of the petitioners that if St. Anthony fails to answer a request, his image may be turned upside-down as punishment for causing disappointment. Worshippers like to caress favoured religious objects and then attempt to transfer their miraculous powers by applying the caressing hand to their own bodies—sometimes to cure trouble in one place, such as face, chest, arms or legs, sometimes to transfer the general good influence. All the churches in the city sell *milagros*—small silver or gold replicas of hearts, limbs, and other parts of the body to be pinned to statues in gratitude for prayers answered.

Hand in hand with the belief in the direct intervention of saints goes a lingering reliance on magical rituals and herbal cures. Such ancient folk medicine, which often has a sound basis in modern pharmacology, meets

Myriad candles flicker in a Mexico City cemetery on the annual Day of the Dead (November 2) as Mexican families, seeking to commune with departed spirits, gather beside tombs of deceased relatives for whom they have brought gifts of food, drink and flowers. On one grave (below), piled with offerings of fruit, sugar cane and loaves, genuine skulls serve as macabre candle-holders.

a very real need; the herbal remedies provide just about the only medical care available to huge numbers of informally employed people who could not begin to pay for private medical care and are not covered by the state welfare scheme, which applies only to those in full-time employment.

Near the Zócalo is the Sonora Market where *curanderos* (native healers) sell not only their herbal cures but lucky charms and all kinds of potions. The mystical wares are varied, to say the least: coloured candles for making a curse or casting a love-spell; magical powders to preserve good health; little packets of wood shavings labelled "To help find lost objects"; hideous *diabolo* (devil fish), dried and shrunken, to cure cancer. There are snake-skins, raccoon tails, squirrel pelts, tortoise shells, starfish, toads and endless other exotic ingredients—each with its own powers.

The truest form of syncretism in Mexico is the survival of pre-Christian religious traditions inextricably fused with Catholic orthodoxy. Some of the older churches still display pagan symbols amid the Christian statuary in the carvings round their doorways. And, during religious festivals, Mexicans still perfume the air with the sickly sweet smell of copal, the resin of various tropical trees that was burnt as incense by the Aztec priests.

One of the most strikingly syncretistic festivals is the festival on November 2, popularly known as the Day of the Dead. It embodies traces of old pagan rites for the comfort of departed spirits, combined with the celebration of the Christian festival of All Souls. As the day approaches, department stores in Mexico City are hung with papier-mâché skeletons, and death becomes a major retail industry. Children merrily clamour for the candy skulls that are piled high in confectioners' shops. Also for sale are death masks, candles of remembrance, special sweet bread called *pan de muerte* (bread of death) baked in the shape of long bones—and, as usual in Mexico City, billions of flowers, especially yellow and orange marigolds which since Aztec times have been considered the favourite flowers of the dead—the *flores de los muertos*.

On the day itself the cemeteries echo with the festive sounds of grave-side parties. Relatives offer food and flowers to the spirits of the departed, tombs are swept and cleaned, and sometimes decorated with black paper flags, ceramic skulls (or sometimes even real ones) and coloured ribbons. Often a picture of the deceased will be prominently displayed, and always candles are lit. Families who prefer to hold the remembrance feast at home hang marigold wreaths over their doors and lay out offerings before makeshift candlelit altars. Sometimes they also lay trails of marigold petals from the street into the house to guide the dead home.

Properly though, the entire day should be spent at the graveside; and this remains the popular custom among the poorer classes of Mexico City, despite efforts by the police to discourage people from taking food and drink into cemeteries. But it is difficult to stop the practice, since it is impossible to guard the full perimeter of every graveyard and

Belief in the supernatural survives in modern Mexico City. At the Sonora Market, near the Zócalo, a "magic store" (right) sells objects— amulets, herbs and even aerosols—for sorcery. Outside, a poster (above) lists available items, such as magic candles and love potions.

prevent picnic baskets from being smuggled over the walls to friends who have passed scrutiny at the main gate.

The Mexican cult of the dead has had many critics. Some foreigners regard it as macabre, even shocking—especially the involvement of children. The Church disapproves of the superstitious practice of putting out food and drink for the dead; and the civic authorities object because the cemeteries are left strewn with litter and late-night drinking often follows, leading to rowdy behaviour. I myself take the view that the dead are best remembered with this kind of fond, festive communion. One Mexican I know has even instructed his poker-playing friends—if they survive him—to hold a game at his grave on the first November 2 after his death, and to deal him a hand of four aces. Such a gesture is very much in keeping with the spirit of the occasion.

In pre-Hispanic times the Aztec year was crowded with festivals marked by processions, music and dancing. So it is today. Fiestas are central to the Mexican way of life. There are hundreds of religious festivals, national holidays and saints' days in Mexico, and even special holidays reserved for different occupations: the day of the mailman, the day of the garbage collector, the day of the news-boy and so on. In addition, many people who have come to live in the capital continue to celebrate the saint's day of their original district or village, so keeping alive their sense of community and identity in the vastness of the city.

The longest of Mexican festivities is Christmas. Traditionally, the celebrations begin on December 16 with the first of nine *posadas* (literally "inns"): nightly re-enactments of Mary and Joseph's search for lodgings in Bethlehem. According to custom, groups of neighbouring families journey from house to house in candlelit procession, knocking on each door and chanting: "In the name of heaven we ask room for the night." Every night, by pre-arrangement, one family in each group takes its turn to admit the inn-seekers and to escort them to the *nacimiento*, a crib set up under a Christmas tree. A party follows with food and drink, singing and dancing. The building of high-rise apartment blocks and condominiums with their lack of community sense has discouraged these festivities in some parts of Mexico City, but innumerable inhabitants still maintain this gloriously sociable custom and so enjoy parties on nine successive nights—the last and liveliest party being held on Christmas Eve.

One Sunday, when I was the dinner guest of a middle-class Mexican family, a university student expressed the view that Spain had contributed very little of lasting value to the development of Mexico. "What is your opinion?" he asked me. As a stranger to the family circle, I was anxious not to say that Spain has been important in two key respects—by giving seemingly innocuous statement of the obvious: "Well, I suppose it is fair to say that Spain has been important in two key respects—by giving Mexico its language and its religion."

I should have known better. In Mexico few such opinions can be expressed so straightforwardly. The student's father, who had just returned from church, looked at me very solemnly. "You are wrong, señor. Quite wrong. It was not the Spaniards who gave us our Christian religion. It was the work of our own lady, the Virgin of Guadalupe." And there, as though guillotined, the discussion ended.

One cannot hope to understand the puzzles of Mexican religion without considering the Virgin of Guadalupe, whose image, dusky and serene, is to be seen everywhere in Mexico City—in factories, at the depots and railway stations, on the dashboards and mirrors of buses and cars, in bars and shops. Every one of these pictures is a representation of the most revered religious relic in Latin America: the miraculous painting of the Virgin, housed in the modern multi-million-peso Basilica of Guadalupe. The story of the miracle—authenticated by Pope Alexander VII in 1663— is known to virtually every Mexican and is accepted by most.

It begins on the morning of December 8, 1531, when a poor Indian peasant by the name of Juan Diego, newly converted to Christianity, was making his way to mass at the Church of Santiago (St. James), Tlatelolco. As he skirted the steep rocky hill of Tepeyac, four miles north of Mexico City's present-day Zócalo, he suddenly heard celestial music and a voice that asked in his native Nahuatl tongue: "Juan, my son, where are you going?" As he replied, explaining that he was going to church, he noticed that the entire hill was flooded with radiant light. Following the voice, he climbed to the summit and, under an arch of blinding sun-rays, saw a

At the festival of the Virgin of Guadalupe, a family lines up before a backdrop showing pictures of the Virgin and of the old and new basilicas dedicated to her.

Disciples of Guadalupe

Every year, on December 12, tens of thousands of Mexicans gather at the new Basilica of Guadalupe—built near the old basilica at Tepeyac, four miles north of the city centre—to celebrate the anniversary of a 16th-Century miracle: the appearance of the Virgin Mary to a simple Indian peasant named Juan Diego. Throughout the day pilgrims stream into the basilica to pay homage to a special image of the Virgin; it is held to be the original portrait that emerged on Juan Diego's mantle in 1531 to confirm his vision. The painting draws pilgrims from all over Latin America, and every devout Mexican Catholic aspires to visit the Virgin's shrine at least once during his lifetime.

On the eve of the festival of Guadalupe, pilgrims who have journeyed by bicycle and on foot camp overnight in the plaza beside the old Basilica of Guadalupe.

A troupe of Conchero dancers entertain pilgrims in the plaza between the old and new basilicas. The Concheros, who wear an image of the Virgin on their backs, belong to a long-established semi-pagan fraternity that worships both the Holy Cross and the four winds. Their colourful costumes and dances are rooted in pre-Christian tribal culture.

vision who informed him that she was the Immaculate Virgin Mary, Mother of the True God.

She told Juan Diego to go at once to the Bishop of Mexico City and explain that it was her wish to have a sanctuary built on the hill so that she could be near her Indian people, to protect and love them. Twice the humble Indian obeyed her command, twice he was turned away by the Spanish Church authorities. Returning to the same site and meeting again with the Virgin, he explained that Fray Juan de Zumarraga, the first Bishop of Mexico City, refused to listen to him unless he was able to bring a convincing sign. The Virgin promised to give Juan Diego a sign the next day.

The following day, December 12, Juan Diego found a field of scented roses blooming on the formerly barren rock at the summit of Tepeyac Hill. At the Virgin's command, he gathered an armful of roses and wrapped them inside his *tilma*, a blue-green mantle woven from the fibres of the maguey cactus. "This is my sign," she said. "Take it to the Lord Bishop and only unfold the cloak when you are in his presence." Juan Diego obeyed and, when he spread his cloak before the Bishop, out fell the roses. Also, imprinted on the inner surface of the empty *tilma* was an image of the Virgin Mary, standing on a crescent moon and surrounded by beams of light. She wore a rose-coloured tunic embroidered with roses and a blue robe dusted with stars. Her head was tilted to one side, her eyes half closed, her expression one of serene compassion. Convinced, the Bishop ordered a chapel to be built for the Virgin at Tepeyac.

It is this picture, on Juan Diego's *tilma*, which now hangs in a golden frame above the altar in the new Basilica of Guadalupe. Guides say the fabric never deteriorates and the colours never fade, but these miraculous qualities are less important to Mexicans than the fact that the Virgin is brown-skinned. Here was a Virgin the conquered Mexican people could claim as their own. Significantly, she had appeared to Juan Diego on the site of a destroyed shrine belonging to an Aztec goddess of fertility, known as Tonantzin (Our Mother). At first the Indians called her La Morena (The Dark One); but now, following the name officially accorded by the Catholic Church, she is universally known as the Virgin of Guadalupe. Why Guadalupe? The most likely explanation ascribes the choice of the name to the great popularity, among the Spanish colonists at the time, of a cult of the Virgin centred on the famous shrine of Guadalupe in Spain. The name of that shrine was simply transferred to the new one.

The cult of the dark Virgin spread quickly across Mexico. When, in 1629, a great flood swamped Mexico City, thousands of people were drowned or killed by falling masonry. To reinforce the people's prayers, the Archbishop had the painting brought down from the chapel on Tepeyac Hill and placed in the Metropolitan Cathedral. Soon afterwards, the rains stopped and the floods subsided: proof, if proof were needed, of the Virgin's power. Her image was returned to Tepeyac with her position as

Many Mexican churches post "retablos": illustrated messages giving thanks for divine aid. The Church of Our Lady of the Remedies in the north-west of the city has an especially large display (above) because the cult of the Virgin centred on this church is associated with healing. A typical message (extreme left) reads: "I thank the Virgin of Remedies for performing the miracle of making my little girl walk after the unpleasant illness of infantile paralysis."

protectress of the city unassailable, and in 1709 a new, much grander church of sandstone and red volcanic rock was built for her at the foot of the hill, to replace the original chapel.

In the 19th Century, a secret report prepared for the Archbishop of Mexico by the eminent historian Don Joaquin Garcia reluctantly concluded that the painting was not miraculous; it was probably the work of a 16th-Century Indian artist from the convent of Tlatelolco. Later the report was leaked; yet it made no difference to the Virgin's status in the eyes of her devoted followers. In 1895 a crown of gold and precious jewels, made in Paris, was suspended over her image. In 1904 the Church of Guadalupe at the base of Tepeyac Hill was elevated to the status of a basilica, and in 1945 Pope Pius XII declared the Virgin "Patroness of the Americas".

Unfortunately the basilica stood on treacherous subsoil and sank deeper year by year, until its sacristy was tilted at a crazy angle. In the 1960s millions of pesos were spent on efforts to jack up the great edifice, but to little avail; and in 1970 the Church decided to build a new basilica to house the Virgin.

Consecrated in 1976, the new building stands across the plaza from the old basilica, which is now closed. It is an enormous circular structure, uncompromisingly modern in design and capable of accommodating more than 10,000 worshippers. From afar it resembles a colossal, green-topped, conical marquee; within, it is rather like a vast concert hall, with pews fanning out in a great arc from the stage-like main altar. The floor is marble, the walls are covered in cedar decorated with gold leaf, and the lighting is so artfully arranged that the interior seems to glow naturally in golden sunlight. Not a single pillar interrupts the wide-angle view from the main entrance.

Many people think that the new shrine is too modern and lacking in dignity. It is so functional in design that it even has a travellator running behind the altar so that the crowds who come to see the Virgin are kept moving as they pass directly below her image—the only picture in the building. But I greatly admire this basilica. It lacks the stately dignity of the old building; on the other hand, it is devoid of Gothic gloom or forbidding solemnity. It is bright and airy—a warm, inviting place where even the humblest Mexicans may feel welcome and at ease.

Every day at least 12 masses are held in the basilica; every week dele-gations arrive from some part of Mexico to pay homage to the Virgin and seek her blessing. December 12, the Virgin of Guadalupe's feast-day, is a day of festivity when all Mexico celebrates the anniversary of her image's miraculous appearance on Juan Diego's cloak, and tens of thousands of pilgrims converge on her shrine, filling the monumental plaza outside the basilica and crowding the streets far beyond. For many it is an occasion for profound piety, for others a prelude to a great fiesta, and for some—folk dancers, photographers, itinerant musicians and hordes of *venda-*

dores of food, souvenirs, brochures and cheap religious trinkets—an outstanding commercial opportunity.

On this day more than any other, the basilica becomes the centre of an extravagantly colourful spectacle. But there are other days of great pageantry. In February every year more than 70,000 men, women and children from the state of Mexico make a pilgrimage to the Virgin, most of them walking for three days from Toluca, their capital, 50 miles from Mexico City. Their arrival on the eve of Toluca Day, February 16, is an astonishing sight. An apparently endless column of dusty pilgrims, divided into some 200 separate groups, each following the banner that bears an image of the Virgin and the name of their particular town or village, winds through the city, halting traffic for an hour or more whenever a major intersection has to be crossed.

Not long ago, I watched this great tide of humanity sweep into the plaza in front of the Basilica of Guadalupe and settle on almost every square foot of the paved area and the grass verges beyond. They unfolded their *petates* (rolled-up mats), set up portable stoves and even pitched tents against the basilica walls. Among the pilgrims were nonagenarians hobbling on sticks and innumerable women carrying babies within their *rebozos* as well as blanket-wrapped loads on their backs. Some of them— those who had started from areas beyond Toluca—had been walking for more than three days; yet many found the immediate strength to shuffle on their knees to the main altar. Some even began their suppliant approach from the far edge of the plaza outside—a laboured journey that added approximately 150 yards and lasted at least an hour as they negotiated the heedless sea of squatters.

I talked to one elderly woman as she emerged smiling from the basilica. Her name was María Pilar Toledano, a widow and grandmother who had taken a week's holiday from the Toluca workroom where she embroidered *sarapes*, blouses and skirts. "I have kept my promise to Our Lady," she explained. "A year ago I promised I would come here to thank God for everything. Now it is done. I feel very tired, but happy."

All around, the pilgrims were preparing to bed down for the night on the cold stone pavement of the plaza. In the gathering gloom, the wind was strengthening and whipping clouds of dust across the square. Dogs were scavenging for scraps of food among the makeshift tents and a loud-speaker blared out announcements about lost children. Señora Toledano was among the luckier pilgrims. With other early arrivals, she had reserved a large doorway in a wall of the nearby old basilica. Here, 15 women had constructed a tent by tying sheets to woodwork above the doors and securing them on the ground with boulders. Some were already preparing a meal of chicken in *mole* on a small charcoal stove.

Towering in the background was the hill of Tepeyac, where it all began. I asked Señora Toledano if she would be making a pilgrimage to the hallowed summit. She rubbed her blistered feet and winced. "It is not necessary," she said. "Only the sacred image in the basilica is important."

Few pilgrims are inspired to visit the Virgin's original sanctuary—but then it is not exactly an inspiring place. The hilltop shrine is a small chapel, dark and narrow, dominated within by an agonized carving of Christ on the cross: a chilling, despairing figure in black wood, with multiple wounds dripping blood from head to foot. Beside the chapel is a small *panteon* (cemetery), notable only for the grave of General Santa Anna. The Virgin's chapel on Tepeyac Hill is the very antithesis of her light-flooded, hope-giving shrine in the square below.

At noon the following day, all the pilgrims assembled on the plaza, standing behind their respective banners, which were now lined up to form a 100-yard-long corridor to the basilica entrance. At 1 o'clock the official delegates filed inside with their banners and took up positions in a huge semicircle facing the sacred painting spotlighted in its golden frame above the altar. Many of the tens of thousands who remained outside to hear the mass relayed by loudspeakers began to sing:

Lady of the Sky, O Queen of Love,
Lodge us, Mother, in your heart.
Sweet Mother, don't go away.
Don't take your eyes off us. . . .

After the mass, Toluca Day reached its breathtaking climax. Again, the multicoloured banners were lined up outside the basilica, this time to salute the departure of the Virgin of Toluca, the largest banner, which bore a reproduction of the Virgin of Guadalupe, set in a frame studded with battery-operated electric lights. As the Virgin of Toluca emerged from the church, borne high on a wooden frame adorned with bouquets of gladioli, thousands of voices united to sing: "Goodbye, Queen of the Heavens! Goodbye, Mother of Jesus! *Adiós! Adiós! Adiós!*"

From the main street leading out of the plaza, I looked back on a panorama of religious rejoicing that is etched indelibly on my mind's eye. In the background towered the green domes of the contrasting basilicas— the new on the left, the old on the right. In the foreground, amid the forest of banners, the thousands of pilgrims were waving farewell as the Virgin of Toluca was borne to a waiting municipal truck with streamers and flowers. "*Adiós! Adiós! Adiós!*" The cries rose to a crescendo. Some cheered. Some wept. A brass band began to play and delegates swung copal-burning censers, filling the air with Aztec perfume. Then, amid a puff of exhaust fumes and the clang-clang accompaniment of a passing trolley-car, the Virgin of Toluca left Mexico City for another year.

Now began the great homeward trek—not on foot this time, but on bicycles unloaded from trucks, on the trucks themselves and, for a fortunate minority, in upholstered coaches. Once home, the pilgrims would attend fiesta parties and relate their memories of the great day.

A Park for All Purposes

Hazily visible through the transparent folds of a tent, two dog-owners attending a competition in the park ponder the finer points of an Afghan hound.

On the gentle slopes of Chapultepec Park—the name derives from the Aztec *chapulin* (grasshopper) and *tepetl* (hill)—the Emperor Moctezuma II once had his summer residence, surrounded by extensive gardens for his private use. Today the park is open to everyone and on an average weekend more than a million visitors take their pleasure among its thousand wooded acres. Most local citizens escape to the park from small, crowded dwellings and, thanks to Mexico City's reliably benevolent weather, they are able to enjoy a very wide range of activities that, in other cities, would typically be held indoors. Visitors who want more than a few hours of peace may get involved in anything from a child's party or a dog show to one of the government-sponsored courses designed to help the unskilled learn a trade, such as woodworking or hairdressing.

Surrounded by dense greenery, sufficient to provide the illusion of life in the wild, campers in an unfrequented glade of the park put up a tent for the day.

Determined to develop a profitable skill, these women attend a park class in hairdressing held on Sundays. The fee for each lesson is a nominal 10 pesos.

Stripped for action under the afternoon sun, a young aficionado side-steps the charge of the bull, ably impersonated by his father, in a Chapultepec grove.

At a children's party held in an area marked out with balloons, a birthday boy uses a wooden pole to smash a hanging piñata—a clay pot filled with sweets and toys

nd decorated with coloured paper to resemble an animal or a cartoon character. As the contents come spilling out, guests scrabble for the prizes on the ground.

A candy-floss seller, one of innumerable park vendors who purvey everything from snacks to balloons and postcards, takes a moment off to try his own wares.

6

Weekends for Unwinding

Now that Mexico has entered the ranks of rapidly industrializing countries, it is fashionable to emphasize the new-found dynamism of the people. Ignorant foreigners are expected to abandon their last cobwebbed images of the Mexican as a work-shy *peon* snoozing in the fingered shade of a giant cactus. In modern Mexico City, such a stereotype bears little relation to reality: for several years offices increasingly have been following an official recommendation to abandon the traditional two- or three-hour afternoon siesta in favour of the *semana inglesa*—"English week"—based on a nine-to-five workday.

Lifestyles change. Traditions change. Values change. But do the basic characteristics of people really change? While recognizing that innumerable inhabitants of the city work very hard indeed, I nevertheless cling to the belief—which I hold is complimentary rather than disparaging —that the majority are, by temperament, ill-suited to the hectic and competitive way of life that modernization has thrust upon them. In the back-street markets, it is still possible to buy wall plaques engraved with the popular sentiment: "*Mañana* is the best tool to save time that was ever invented." But for many Mexicans the words may sound a regretful note: there is no *mañana* escape for millions of workers caught up in the increasingly complex demands of their changing city, and their frustration shows. It shows in the desperation of commuters struggling to enter already jam-packed Metro trains, in the foot-shuffling impatience of would-be bus travellers faced with an interminable wait, and in the stony faces of motorists who drive with a cold-blooded aggression that is liable to boil up into uncontrolled fury at the challenging hoot of a horn. (In Mexico City, it is by no means extraordinary for drivers to come to blows.)

In the late 1970s, the mayor of Mexico City, Carlos Hank Gonzalez, described his city as a "labyrinth of anxiety"—a variation on the title of Octavio Paz's famous study of the Mexican character, *The Labyrinth of Solitude*. More recently, a leading Mexican publisher catalogued for me the many social and environmental sicknesses of his city and concluded: "Life here is unpleasant whichever way you look at it. A city that is destroying itself generates destructive emotions—impatience, bad temper, aggression, egoism, loneliness, boredom, disgust and impotence."

But I disagree with this overwhelmingly condemnatory view. There is another—and to my mind a truer—side to Mexican responses. I see the typical Mexican—risky though it may be to claim that there is such a thing—as a person endowed with a very considerable appetite for

Accompanied by a trumpeter and a violinist, a mariachi vocalist hits a high note in the popular Tenampa Saloon on the Plaza Garibaldi. The mariachis are musicians who play in small bands typically composed of a singer or two, guitarists, violinists, and usually a trumpeter or trombonist. Traditionally mariachis wear silver-studded black suits with long bow ties, but some—like this singer—choose an updated version of the time-honoured costume.

leisure and for the simple pleasures of life, a person who is happier if he works to live, rather than lives to work. There is, correspondingly, another side to Mexico City, an infinitely rewarding side that reveals itself whenever its citizens have the opportunity to be themselves—to indulge their appetites for leisure and pleasure, or simply to live at the instinctive, easy pace that seems to suit them so well. This is the Mexico City I love—the city that re-emerges every weekend.

The unwinding begins slowly. On Saturday, a few factories and offices operate through the morning, while retail businesses continue at full blast all day. But by Sunday, the relaxation of tensions is complete; indeed, if every day could be Sunday, Mexico City would qualify as one of the most enchanting cities on earth. All at once, this hectic metropolis puts on an entirely new face. The physical change is striking enough: a sharpening of focus as the city casts off its *sarape* of smog; the sound of bird-song above the traffic's muted roar. But it is the change of mood, of human behaviour patterns, that is really so remarkable. The big city, one feels, has been silently occupied in the night by an entirely new race of relaxed and smiling country folk.

Sunday in Mexico City can mean many different things: attending morning mass, a midday outing to the *charreada* (Mexico's unique version of the rodeo), a long lunch, a late afternoon at the bullfights, an evening at the cinema. But above all, it is a day for family outings, for visits to relatives, or picnics in the parks and outlying pine forests. (Because the weather of Mexico City is almost always good—or at least predictable— outdoor excursions can be confidently planned.)

To appreciate the true glory of Mexico City on a Sunday the newcomer has only to explore the area that is both heart and lungs to the metropolis: Chapultepec Park. This is, in my opinion, the finest park in the world— more beautiful than the Bois de Boulogne, more eventful than New York's Central Park, more charming than London's St. James's Park. By com- bining the best features of those famed islands of greenery and throwing in a touch of Disneyland, one might, I suppose, create a rival to Chapultepec Park. But it would only be in the physical sense. The essential charm of this thousand-acre wonderland can never be duplicated. It belongs to the Mexican people, by way of the kaleidoscope of colourful sights and sounds that they themselves create.

On any day, Chapultepec Park is an area of infinite fascination. It is, after all, the park that has everything: the stately castle that was once the palace of the Emperor Maximilian, five other museums, six theatres, three boating lakes, three bandstands, two miniature railways, two roller-skating rinks, a zoo, a flower market, botanical gardens, a fairground, a practice bullring, a polo field, children's playgrounds, restaurants, spectacular fountains and a grove of centuries-old *ahuehuetes* (cypress trees) towering as high as 200 feet, the survivors of forests that once covered the

Fortunes on Tap

For many of the city's inhabitants, the chance to win a major National Lottery prize is a constant dream. Tickets are sold everywhere by street vendors, and a draw is held every Monday, Wednesday and Friday at 8 p.m. in the National Lottery Building. Each time more than 1,300 prizes, including one worth more than $200,000, are to be won. Boys in uniform call out the winning numbers and corresponding prizes. One boy, operating a lever, releases from a huge revolving cage a ball inscribed with a number. From a smaller cage, another boy releases a ball indicating the amount of that prize. Every boy is retired as soon as his voice breaks and loses its quality of innocence.

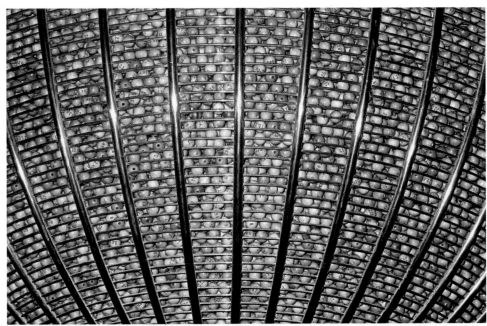

One ball among those in the cage is worth millions of pesos.

The turn of a tap releases a ball with a winning number.

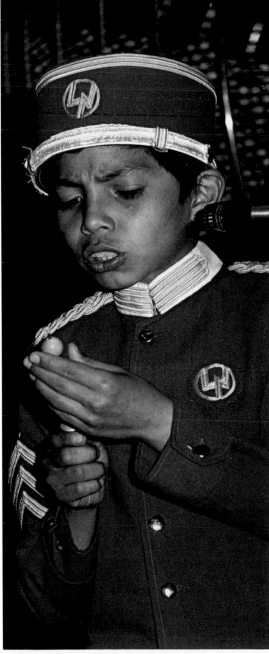

A boy cries out a lucky number.

surrounding mountainsides, However, on Sundays—and to a lesser degree on Saturdays—Chapultepec Park takes on an added dimension as upwards of half a million people gather to sample its pleasures.

The scene becomes a glorious carnival of life, spread thickly here, thinly there, over a parkland almost a mile long from east to west, and a full mile wide at one point. Wherever one wanders, colourful sights arrest the eye: a column of Mexican *charro* riders, ramrod straight and resplendent in their traditional gear of sombrero, short jacket and tight trousers as they silently ride the bridle-paths; a woman bearing a caged bird that tells fortunes by picking out cards from a selection ranged in front of it; a vendor roped to a rainbow cluster of gas-filled balloons and weighted down by festoons of rubber balls attached to his waist; and other pedlars selling multicoloured whirligigs and kites, bright-patterned blankets and shawls, candy-floss and *chicharrones*—pieces from a crisp-hard pork crackling, almost sombrero-sized, topped with chili paste and lime.

Almost as varied is the medley of sounds: the ting-a-ling of the ice-cream vendor's bell, the clang-clang of horse-drawn carriages, the dap-dap of soccer balls bouncing on pathways, the laughter of children, the grinding of an old-fashioned waltz on a hand organ, the oom-pah-pah of a small brass band, and the screams from the *Montaña Rusa* (Russian Mountain)—the gigantic roller-coaster that dominates the fairground. There is activity everywhere—people strolling, cycling, boating, watching open-air theatricals, listening to concerts, picnicking and playing chess. But it is *relaxed* activity. Although one might see young men engaged in a vigorous game of volley-ball, or small children swarming over the playground equipment, most people eschew anything more strenuous than a gentle row on the lakes.

One of the park's most popular attractions is Maximilian's old palace crowning Chapultepec Hill and containing the National Museum of History. It may be approached by spiralling pathways—a delightful, un-demanding 15-minute climb. There are always a few people drifting quietly up—as much for the superb view as for the reminders of the past exhibited in the museum. But, significantly, most Mexicans will not make the approach on foot. Instead, they take the one-peso bus ride that winds round the back of the hill, or—more usually—they stand for as long as one hour in the queue for an antiquated elevator that is built into the rock and delivers its passengers inside the castle itself. The elevator is, ludi-crously, limited to six passengers per trip plus the operator who collects the half-peso fares. But no one complains about the slowness of this service. Here—and in Chapultepec Park as a whole, for that matter—one feels that everyone has miraculously switched off all the impatience and ill temper that characterize weekday life in Mexico City.

The park has another utopian aspect. Because first-class recreational and cultural facilities have been provided for people of diverse interests

Three elephants solemnly perform their tricks in Chapultepec Park's zoo, which houses some 2,000 species of mammals, reptiles and birds. The zoo occupies the site where once stood the private aviary of Emperor Moctezuma II.

and of all ages and, because so many of the attractions are free of charge, there is no obvious appearance of a society divided into haves and have-nots. The communal spirit is perhaps best exemplified by the Casa del Lago (House on the Lake) Cultural Centre, which includes a theatre, library, open-air auditorium and study centre. Its range of free entertainments, conferences and lectures is impressive enough; still more impressive are its educational programmes. Every Sunday, several hundred Mexicans gather at picnic tables beside the lake to receive tuition in a score of different subjects: sculpture, woodwork, dressmaking, watch-repairing, weaving, boat-modelling, doll-making, hairdressing, needle-work, flower arrangement, electrical repairwork, English. The teachers are volunteers who give their services free or, in some cases, make a minimal charge. The students are adults from all walks of life—shop-keepers, factory workers, labourers and, most numerous of all, young mothers seeking a part-time skill to boost the family income.

For children, Chapultepec Park is a paradise. Far and wide, while exploring the park, one sees paper chains and multicoloured balloons strung between trees to mark off a great square of grass; they indicate that the area has been commandeered by a family for a children's party. Some are simple picnics for a dozen or so relatives and friends; more often, they are elaborate affairs with food and drink for perhaps 40 people or more, in addition to organized games with prizes. But, whatever the scale, every party has the same climax—a happy hysteria contrived by smashing one or two *piñatas*, large representations of animals or cartoon characters traditionally made by applying bright paper and cardboard to a pot of clay. Everywhere, *piñatas* are suspended from trees in readiness. Later, blindfolded children will swing at them with a stick until the clay pots finally disintegrate and disgorge their contents—candy, fruit, peanuts, sticks of sugar cane, and perhaps some plastic toys.

One Sunday, around noon, I wandered across to a party being held in a section of the park known as the Parque Rosario Castellanos, a par-ticularly favoured spot because it has an adventure playground nearby and, more valuably, a number of tree-stump seats and barbecues per-manently fixed in concrete. A clown-cum-conjurer was entertaining some 30 children seated cross-legged on the grass below two high-hanging *piñatas* representing the comic-strip characters Snoopy and Tweetie-Pie. Nearby, as many adults were gathered around large trestle-tables bending under the weight of a banquet: a multi-tiered birthday cake, trays of salad, sweet potatoes, strips of grilled beef, chicken *tortas* (bread rolls con-taining meat, vegetables and chili sauce), a bowl of punch, crates of soft drinks and enormous glass jugs of *jamaica,* a popular soft beverage home-made by boiling and sweetening the red petals of the jamaica flower. At a barbecue several women were cooking *tacos*: snacks made by frying *tortillas*—Mexico's round flat pancakes of unleavened maize—that

A lakeside stage in Chapultepec Park provides a magically appropriate setting for an open-air, evening performance of Tchaikovsky's ballet "Swan Lake".

have been filled with bean paste, shredded meat and red or green tomatoes, flavoured with chili sauce.

A young man in the party invited me to have a drink. "Everyone is welcome," he said. "My boy Francisco is three years old today." An engineer, he lived with his family some seven miles away, near Ciudad Satélite (Satellite City), a vast, new, middle-class development built on the outskirts of Mexico City and markedly American in style, with its enormous, closed-in shopping precincts, supermarkets and underground car parks. He explained that they had begun to prepare for Francisco's party more than a month ago. This morning, long before dawn, he and a cousin had gone ahead to reserve the best site.

Friends had been arriving since 7.30 a.m. and the party would continue until at least 5 p.m. The cost? "About 3,000 to 4,000 pesos ($140 to $180)," said the proud father. "I don't know exactly because we hadn't reckoned on the clown." The clown wandered from party to party, charging 300 pesos for a 45-minute performance and, once the children had spotted him, it was only the most hard-hearted or hard-up of parents who could ignore their persistent pleas for a show. "But it's worth every peso," the father continued. "Our house is much too small for a party. Here we can have as many friends as we like. We don't get the furniture spoilt, and the children are much happier in the open air. It's the kind of party they remember all their lives."

The French essayist Charles Flandrau, observing in 1911 the serenity and well-mannered obedience of Mexican children, suggested that all the world's children should be required to be Mexican until the age of 15. If they could all have access to Chapultepec Park, I would whole-heartedly agree. Only once, during many visits to the park, have I seen a child in tears. It happened at the Periferico: a track where children ride tricycles around a miniature version of Mexico City's main *periferico* or inner ring road. After queueing for some 15 minutes, a small girl had been refused entry because she was only $36\frac{1}{2}$ inches tall; for safety reasons, tricycles were restricted to children between 37 inches and 41 inches tall. As she walked away, quietly sobbing, bystanders cried "Shame!" It was more than the gateman could bear. He called the girl back, and everyone cheered.

South-east of Chapultepec Park, the city has another famous open-air pleasure centre—Xochimilco, the outlying aquatic playground where the last faint echoes of the Aztec city's floating gardens or *chinampas* survive. At first sight, this labyrinth of canals and small plots of land can seem absurdly overrated. The word Xochimilco (pronounced zochee-MEEL-ko) is a sweet-sounding Nahuatl word meaning "the place where the flowers grow". Unfortunately its banks do not always give quite such a flowery impression as the name might lead you to expect, although there is a market always offering a rich variety of plants and saplings for sale. But

Xochimilco's appeal to visitors nowadays rests more on its aquatic pleasures than its floral charm.

The canals themselves, between 10 and 50 feet wide, are muddy and stagnant, and darkened by the shade cast by the *sauces huejotes*—tall, straight, indigenous trees that look very much like poplars. Unlike Chapultepec Park, Xochimilco is not a place to which one longs to return again and again. Yet, in a curious way, it is an even more striking example of the recreational flair of the Mexican people. Here they have succeeded in creating a major weekend resort. At weekends, day-tripping hordes bring to this sleepy suburb a scene of delightfully organized chaos. Thousands of Mexicans and tourists are poled along the ancient Aztec-made waterways in flat-bottomed boats painted red and yellow, with zinc awnings of blue. The boats are so crowded together that they often bridge the water in the main channels. And, always enhancing the joyful confusion, there is a never-ending stream of hucksters in punts and canoes: sellers of bright-coloured *sarapes* and *rebozos*, itinerant musicians and photographers; and, most numerous of all, the boatmen and women offering soft drinks, canned beer, *tortillas, tacos, tortas*, fried chicken, strips of pork, coconuts, fruits and countless other snacks. Xochimilco is a place to be enjoyed as one of a group of revellers—eating, drinking and singing as they glide along, and generally surrendering to the fiesta atmosphere that is created whenever Mexicans congregate in a great multitude.

The market-places of Mexico City, swarming with people at the weekends, tend to generate the same sort of spirit—and their animated crowds seem to me a more convincing evocation of the vanished glories of Tenochtitlan than Xochimilco's murky canals. When the conquistadors came to Tenochtitlan more than four centuries ago, they were—in the words of the chronicler Bernal Díaz—"astounded at the great number of people and the quantities of merchandise" in the market-place. After a visit to any of Mexico City's teeming markets, I know how they felt.

These markets—some in covered market-halls, some out of doors—are as much an entertainment as places of commerce. A special attraction, for example, is the flea market held every Sunday morning at La Lagunilla (Little Lake), an area a few blocks north of the Plaza Garibaldi. The only "lake" to be seen is an ocean of second-hand junk and mostly inexpensive knick-knacks—no place for serious shopping. Nevertheless, it remains a magnet for Mexicans with only a few pesos to spend: a social concourse where they can engage in good-humoured banter and bargaining, and crowd together amid some 900 stalls of infinite variety. "That's it," a vendor cheerfully cries, "keep together and share your fleas! And don't forget to watch your pockets!" Behind one stall, an old man dressed up like Pancho Villa offers rusty, twisted strips of ironmongery called "rifles of the Revolution"; at another, a Mexican garage mechanic sells table cigarette-lighters that he has ingeniously created out of old carburettors;

In the suburb of Xochimilco, 12 miles south of the city centre, multicoloured punts crowd the narrow waterways first created centuries ago by the Aztecs.

at still another, a stallkeeper openly flourishes his illegal copies of an American sex magazine.

Another weekend street market is situated only a few blocks north of the Zócalo in the crowded streets of Tepito. A Tepito resident told me that "anyone who enters Tepito immediately feels hotter"—the result, he claimed, of so much bodily heat generated in a half-mile-square district of approximately 100,000 inhabitants, many of whom sleep eight to a room. Much the same effect can be felt in its market, which is so crowded at weekends that one is able to move along at a rate of only about a hundred yards an hour. Unlike La Lagunilla, many street-stalls here sell so-called "imported" goods of dubious origin—much of it contraband—brand-new and displayed in a mad miscellany. There are toys beside plumbing accessories, jewellery alongside crockery, caged birds and *santos* (images of saints), leather handbags, radios, clothing, *piñatas*, rosaries—a jumble of almost everything from nails to kitchen sinks. Most goods are below standard price, but the ritual of histrionic haggling is always observed.

In some ways, the most impressive markets of all are those selling food —notably La Merced, the city's main food distribution centre, occupying several blocks east of the Zócalo. Foreigners gape in amazement at the astonishing range of produce there, and wonder at the natural richness of a country that gave the Old World so many new foods—including avocados, chocolate, peanuts, squash, tomatoes, vanilla and turkey.

The food that looks so enticing on the market-stalls is, of course, even more tempting when transformed into one of the countless characteristically Mexican dishes. Centuries-old forms of food still predominate despite the ever-growing number of American-style cafeterias, hamburger joints and pizza parlours that appeal chiefly to the aspiring middle classes.

Corn, in the shape of the omnipresent *tortilla*, is the most important food; next in importance is chili—either the chili peppers themselves or a paste made by grinding or pounding them—followed closely by beans and tomatoes. On this seemingly narrow base, the Mexicans have developed a culinary repertoire of astonishing range—though not quite so astonishing when you realize that they have some 50 species of beans alone and more than 140 varieties of chili, differing from each other greatly in size and colour, and most dramatically in flavour.

Much as I love Mexican food, I am less tempted by some of the eating environments to be found in the city's less fashionable quarters. As a weak-minded weight-watcher, I have found that the best antidote to overeating is to visit the monumental public dining-hall that fronts on to the Plaza Garibaldi. Here, under one roof, in an area the size of a football field, thousands of Mexicans may be seen eating at open stalls that offer the most bewildering array of cooked foods imaginable. If one sought to design a vegetarian's hell, this would serve as a perfect model—a display of steaming hunks of animal flesh stretching into the distance as far as the

On a street corner near the old Basilica of Guadalupe, a trained canary picks out a card that will tell the fortune of a passer-by who has paid its owner a few pesos. Such sidewalk attractions are found in Mexico City wherever people tend to gather.

eye can see. But Mexicans like eating this way. They like to be able to pick and choose from a thousand and one ready-made dishes. The prices are moderate, which you cannot say for some of the city's modern hamburger bars. Above all—weekdays and weekends alike—the customers like the communal atmosphere and colourful confusion of a dining-hall that has more than a hundred unpartitioned stalls—an open-plan design that also applies in the adjoining, very public *excusados* (toilets).

For Mexicans, eating constitutes an integral part of the concept of pleasure; but it is also an activity that—because of many subtle differences in flavouring—feeds the spirit of adventure as well as the appetite. The ordinary Mexican may not be able to afford the gourmet's delight of discovering an especially appetizing dish in a restaurant. On the other hand, he may derive enormous satisfaction simply from finding a stall that turns out *tacos* seasoned exactly to his taste.

As long ago as 1906, an English traveller commented: "The Mexican eats as opportunity occurs and, as opportunity is incessantly offered, he is always eating." Certainly it is true that wherever you encounter a large assembly of people in weekend Mexico City—at the *charreadas* or bull-fights, in the parks or street markets—so you will almost always find food-stalls close at hand.

The other most striking feature of Mexico City's recreational life—and the one I most admire—is music. I could no more visualize this city without music than imagine Mexican cooking without chilies. It is virtually

A popular weekend attraction is the Sunday morning "Thieves' Market": the open-air flea mart (right) north of the Zócalo. Here bargain-hunting Mexicans enjoy haggling over prices and rummaging among some 900 stalls strewn with an amazing jumble of goods (above)—from vases and watches to ceramics and clocks.

mandatory for occasions of importance—fiestas, state ceremonials, birthday and saint's-day parties, weddings and group outings.

Music has always been a vital component of Mexican life. In Aztec times, Tenochtitlan resounded with martial music played on flutes, flageolets, whistles, rattles and drums; and every citizen was instructed in ceremonial singing and dancing. No celebration could begin without the beating of a drum—usually a *huehuetl*, a hollowed-out log topped with deer or jaguar skin. The mournful thunder of the largest of drums, the snakeskin-covered *tlepanhuehuetl*, signalled the beginning of war or human sacrifice. Great conch shells served as trumpets to summon citizens to public assemblies or launch them on battle charges.

Nowadays, in Mexico City, music is still vital: a source of emotional nourishment that—when you can hear it over the din of the traffic—automatically raises your spirits. The sounds of itinerant musicians are heard on the streets and in the parks: the clip-clopping beat of the lone *marimba* player punching out notes on his wooden xylophone, the liquid melody rippling from a Veracruzian harp, the throbbing beat of a humpbacked, bass *guitarron*, or the lively twang of a ukelele-like *jarana*. At Xochimilco, the presence of so many itinerant musicians is an essential element of the fiesta mood. In the 50,000-seat Plaza Mexico, the largest bullring in the world, it is the dramatic thunder of trumpets and drums that raises the pulse before the entrance of *el toro*.

But, for me, music in Mexico City has its supreme, most exciting expression in the playing of the *mariachis*, those strolling players immediately identifiable by the traditional costume of *muy macho* tight black trousers with a row of silver buttons down each leg, high leather boots, black velvet jackets also with silver decorations, ruffled white shirts and sombreros. The name *mariachi* is plausibly believed to be a corrupted form of the French word *mariage*, originating in the early 1860s when servants from French-owned *haciendas* ran into town shouting *"Mariage! Mariage!"*, to summon musicians to play at a wedding feast. By tradition, the *mariachis* originated in the city of Guadalajara, but they have migrated to all parts of the country, and there are groups in most towns. Mexico City has an estimated 6,000 *mariachis*, playing in parks, plazas and restaurants, at festivals and sporting events, or wherever their hired services may be required. Usually, a group will consist of six to eight players—perhaps three guitarists, three violinists and a trumpeter or two—and every *mariachi* worthy of that name will have hundreds of songs in his repertoire: stirring *ranchero* (cowboy) songs; ballads about the heroes of the Revolution, about cockfighting and bullfighting; and, in greatest variety of all, songs of romance.

The sight and sound of several hundred musicians—both *mariachis* and other street performers—playing and singing after nightfall in the Plaza Garibaldi is an unforgettable experience. But it is the late-night serenades of the *mariachis* that I love best: the conspiratorial atmosphere as they quietly assemble beneath the window of an unsuspecting señorita; the whispered instructions and gentle tuning-up in a dark, deserted street; and then the dramatic piercing of the night air as soft guitars and high-pitched trumpets accompany the soaring voice of a lead tenor delivering—more often than not—the gentle, beseeching refrain of *"Despierta!"*:

> *Wake up, sweet love of my life. Wake up!*
> *If you are asleep, listen to my voice vibrate beneath your window.*
> *In this song I'm giving my soul to you.*
> *Forgive me for interrupting your sleep, but I couldn't help it,*
> *And this very night I came to tell you:*
> *I love you.*

There is a curiously haunting quality about many of these love-songs that is unique to Mexico—a mestizo quality that combines Spanish melody and Mexican melancholy. There is also an exquisite mellifluousness in the Spanish-Mexican words which translation (sadly) destroys. Usually *mariachis* will perform six or seven ballads in a serenade, and they have songs to fit every romantic circumstance: songs for new love, tender love, passionate love, jealous love, and for desperate love ("Hear me, my dearest, I will fight till I win you if it takes a hundred years"). Very occasionally, too, they may sing songs of rejected love, which may be spiced with enough malice to bring forth an outraged father. Still other songs, like the beautiful *"La Chancla"* (The Old Shoe), may resound with prideful, macho defiance:

> *I love if I'm loved; I forget if I'm forgotten,*
> *I have just one pride: I beg to no one.*
> *When I throw away an old shoe, I don't pick it up again.*

Predominantly, however, it is a gloriously romantic tradition; one that most Mexican women seem to welcome on its own extravagant terms. A few years ago I talked to the late Juanito Mendoza, a former strolling player who had risen to become one of Mexico's most celebrated singers. He recalled that, in his youth, he had been hired by a lawyer who paid him 3,000 pesos ($140) to take a singing trio all the way to Monterrey, 430 miles north of Mexico City. "It was the most curious serenade I can remember. We were driven in the darkness to a huge building, and outside we started to play a love-song. Suddenly, lights came on everywhere. And in every window we could see the faces of nuns. The place was a convent! We were serenading a novice preparing to take her vows! Three times we went to the convent, giving serenades of 30 minutes each. One year later, the girl was released from her vows. She married the lawyer."

Mexico City's night-life has most of the attractions that one associates with a large capital city, from concerts and recitals to restaurants and night-clubs. But one feature continues to surprise foreign visitors: the extraordinary popularity of the cinema (mainly showing Mexican and American films). Since the 1960s, box-office revenues have been rising by tens of millions of pesos annually—a phenomenal rate of increase in a city where more than 85 per cent of homes have six-channel television. I know of no other city where the cinema has boomed so spectacularly alongside television. The phenomenon can be largely explained by the Mexicans' love of escapist entertainment and their predilection for going out in the evening. But there are other, less obvious, contributory factors which have wider significance. First, cinema prices are cheap enough for the young to afford—and Mexico City has probably the youngest population of any capital city in the world. Approximately 50 per cent of its inhabitants are under 20 years of age, and, unless there is a sudden dramatic change in migration patterns, the percentage of young people within the city will remain unusually high.

Secondly, girls are liable to be subject to considerable moral restraint as long as they live with their parents. Of all Mexico City's late-night attractions it is fair to say that the cinema and a rather limited range of theatre represent almost the only acceptable evening activities for women without an approved male escort—acceptable, that is, to parents. Once or twice a week, secretaries and shop assistants may chaperone each other to the cinema after work. It is also very common practice for young women to say that they have been to the cinema with a girlfriend, when actually they have been out with a boy. And, even then, they need to have seen the film at some time or another to make their alibi stick. For women, together or alone, the only real alternative—and one that has become increasingly popular with young people in Mexico City—is to spend an evening in one of the *peñas* (coffee bars) where folk music from many Latin American countries can be heard.

Although Mexican women were not given the vote until as late as 1952, their position has become much freer since then. Nowadays many women are prominent in professional and public life, and have achieved much the same level of emancipation as successful, educated women in any Western capital. Nevertheless, in many ways, society remains strongly male-orientated—a fact that becomes especially apparent as one explores urban night-life beyond the central, touristy zone. The *pulquerías*—traditional establishments serving *pulque*, the milky, fermented juice of the maguey plant that Mexicans have drunk for centuries—usually have separate sections for women, and there are even some *pulquerías* for women only; while the unpretentious, neighbourhood café-bars called *cantinas* represent bastions of almost exclusively male social life. Evening sports events, such as floodlit soccer or *jai alai*—the name by which the Basque game of *pelota* is known in Latin America—are principally of masculine appeal. And, strictly at the working-class level, there are a number of popular entertainments that are theoretically open to both

Seeking an instant evening meal, Mexicans crowd into a vast eating-hall on the Plaza Garibaldi where independently run stalls offer a wide variety of dishes.

sexes but which, in reality, tend to exclude women by virtue of their underlying macho-based conception.

A striking example of such masculine entertainment in Mexico City is nightly vaudeville, a crude mixture of comic sketches, variety acts and explicit strip-tease. I first attended one of these shows at the Apolo Theatre, in an unfashionable district only five blocks east of the Zócalo. Immediately I felt as though I were back in the 1940s, attending a camp entertainment staged for British Army occupation troops in Germany. The scene and atmosphere were much the same: a "theatre" that looked like an aircraft hangar equipped with a stage and hard-backed chairs; and a vociferous, working-class audience composed of approximately 800 men and no more than 20 women.

The two-hour show began with an elaborately costumed "Hello Dolly" number, the curtain-raising appetizer for the salad-without-dressing to follow. The main sketch of the evening—exceedingly coarse though often hilarious—involved a schoolteacher conducting a biology class for retarded adults with the aid of a live nude model; and the only brief relief from acts with sexual overtones was provided by an illusionist who made his female assistant disappear. "Magnificent!" a man in the audience cried. "I'm going to bring my mother-in-law." And everyone roared.

Audience participation was clearly half the fun of the fair. The customers were paying 40 pesos a head not only to look and listen, but also for the pleasure of vying with one another in shouting out vulgar witticisms and for the excitement of egging on the ambitious few who, like bullfighters darting in and out to place their own *banderillas*, sallied forth in attempts to reach up and plant kisses on naked ladies at the front of the stage.

Artistically, the shows represent little more than graffiti brought to life; but at least they are totally honest and uninhibited in their blatant vulgarity, devoid of the smutty, raincoated furtiveness that is the pathetic mark of strip clubs in so many great cities. Here, instead, one sees further evidence of the Mexican inclination towards pleasure taken on a large, communal scale. Furthermore, the strip-tease vaudeville could arguably be regarded as a desirable emotional outlet for the fires of machismo, the private volcano that smoulders perpetually inside the Mexican male and that may at any time erupt into a savage expression of frustration, defiance, jealousy or overweening pride.

It was the Mexican author Armando Ramirez who first told me about the most curious macho entertainment: the "Prostitutes' Ball". I had seen Mexico City's lower-class nightclubs where "hostesses", varying from teenagers to grandmothers, charged 10 pesos a dance and received a small percentage of the price of any drinks they could hustle customers to buy. But this was something more unusual: a nightly dance in Tepito that was restricted to men without female companions and to prostitutes who paid a 50-peso cloakroom fee and a further 50 pesos if they left with

Wearing a costume based on pre-Hispanic ceremonial attire, a male dancer of the renowned Ballet Folklorico recreates an ancient dance in a spectacular review of the country's cultural heritage. The company performs all the year round in the Palace of Fine Arts while a sister company frequently tours the world.

a customer before 1 a.m., closing time. Intrigued, I asked Armando if he would join me on a visit to the ball one night.

At the time I was staying with my Argentinian friend Roberto Donadi and his beautiful Mexican wife Guadalupe. They were equally intrigued, and wanted to see the dance for themselves. But, of course, it was impossible to take Guadalupe and so it was agreed that Roberto should go without her. Her dark, supremely expressive eyes showed disappointment —and very clear warning signals to Roberto—as this exclusive, all-male expedition took shape. Normally, Roberto would not have dreamt of leaving her at home in such circumstances. But on this occasion we had secretly worked out a strategy in advance. We would pay only a cursory visit to the Prostitutes' Ball and then hire a group of *mariachis* to give Guadalupe a serenade.

It was 11 p.m. when we arrived in Tepito. We had arranged to meet Armando—Tepito-born and bred and the son of a one-time featherweight boxing champion—on his home ground. When he turned up, he was accompanied by a somewhat mysterious youth called Fernando who hid behind sun-glasses and always spoke in whispers. Fernando, it emerged, was a fairly regular visitor to the local dance-hall. "You want to be careful," he whispered. "I once picked up a beautiful girl there and when we got outside I discovered she was a boy." Armando advised us to walk down the centre of the street in order to minimize any danger from muggers lurking in doorways.

Contrary to our expectations, the Prostitutes' Ball was remarkably well ordered. Approximately a hundred men and at least an equal number of unescorted women were present. The hall contained a dance floor illuminated by flashing multicoloured lights and surrounded by tables and chairs. There was a bar at one end; at the other end was a stage on which a mini-skirted, all-girl brass band was belting out Latin American rhythms. We grabbed a ringside table and ordered the mandatory drinks.

On the dance floor, a fascinating ritual was being enacted. The majority of prostitutes, surprisingly young and attractive, wore off-the-shoulder cotton dresses or satin blouses that slipped lower and lower as each three-minute dance progressed. With remarkable precision, this manoeuvre was so contrived that each dance usually ended with dress or blouse tantalizingly poised on the brink of total exposure. At that point, the male partner was required to pay his 10 pesos. Hopefully, of course, he would be sufficiently stimulated to request a second dance or perhaps to offer 250 to 500 pesos for a more prolonged duet in the neighbouring brothel.

Within an hour, one empty bottle of over-priced brandy told us that it was time to take our departure. "We have to arrange a serenade," Roberto explained to the others.

Shortly after midnight we arrived in the Plaza Garibaldi, where some 30 or 40 *mariachi* groups were playing for passers-by or for couples who pulled up in cars on their way home from theatre, cinema or restaurant. After some spirited bargaining, we hired an eight-man group called Los Galleros de Mexico (the Cockfighters of Mexico), and they piled into two cars to follow us to the Donadi apartment. For a fee of 1,300 pesos they were to sing six love-songs, beginning their recital in traditional style with the gentle wooing of *"Despierta!"*.

All was dark, deserted and silent as we quietly assembled on the sidewalk directly below Guadalupe's third-floor bedroom window. Instructions were whispered, guitars gently strummed. And then, suddenly, in response to an opening chord, the voice of the lead singer launched into the verses with astonishing power. *"Despierta, dulce amor de mi vida. Despierta!"* (Wake up, sweet love of my life. Wake up!).

After two extra choruses of *"Despierta!"*, there was still not a glimmer of light from Guadalupe's window. The street was silent again. "Perhaps she's out with another boyfriend?" one *mariachi* joked. "Are you sure she's sleeping up there? Okay, let's see if she appears for the second song. Would you like *'Paloma querida'* (Darling dove)? Right! Here we go."

Seconds later, a light flashed on. And there, framed in the window above, was a picture of classic Mexican beauty and elegance. Guadalupe had indeed timed her entrance to perfection. She wore a flower in her raven hair and the smile of all the angels on her lips and in her deep-brown eyes. She blew Roberto a kiss. Then she threw down a single rose. The *mariachis* cheered. A trumpeter sounded a high-pitched, celebratory fanfare. It was a moment of pure magic—the kind of heartfelt magic that lingers on and, at once, makes the harsh weekday realities of Mexico City dissolve into nothingness.

Geometry to Live By

In the spacious Plaza Insurgentes a circular Metro station building gives an off-centre accent, balanced by the orange oblong of an entertainment marquee.

Mexico City, with its vast and sprawling bulk, is an apparently unpromising place to look for purity of form and line—at least for the observer on the ground. But in this set of photographs, Harald Sund has taken views from various heights and has concerned himself with the underlying abstractions of shape, colour and spatial relations; his disciplined perception has elicited from the confused and majestic city this remarkable portfolio of satisfyingly coherent patterns. Some of them were created by the builders of historic monuments, the architects of model housing developments or the engineers of great thoroughfares, others result from the accidental conjunction of shapes and colours in daily life. But still others come simply from the photographer's choice of the one critical moment when a transitory pattern emerges, never to be repeated.

At Columbus Circle, one of the main intersections on Reforma, a build-up of waiting traffic adds an asymmetrical element of colour to the geometric layout.

Near Chapultepec Park fountains play in the traffic circles of a freeway interchange that is transformed by distance into a swirling abstract design.

Gazing eastwards towards the city centre, the angel on the Monument of National Independence presides over another of Reforma's imposing crossroads.

In an eastern district of Mexico City, the tarpaulins that shade the stalls mark with a rough patchwork cross the shape of a weekly street-corner market.

A suburban estate creates a series of diminutive, communal courtyards in an interlocking pattern of concrete.

Hillside houses near Satellite City become an exercise in vertical and sloping planes, punctuated by the metallic capsules of rooftop water tanks.

On a broad mosaic pavement beside the Palace of Fine Arts, the small figures of a woman and her child contribute a fleeting dash of colour— vivid in the city's constant bright sunlight—to the muted half-tones of a sea of perfect circles.

Bibliography

Atkin, Ronald, *Revolution! Mexico 1910-20.* Macmillan & Co. Ltd., London, 1969.

Bernal, Ignacio, *Mexico Before Cortez: Art, History, Legend.* Doubleday & Co. Inc., New York, 1963.

Braasch, Barbara J., ed., *Sunset Travel Guide to Mexico.* Lane Publishing Co., Menlo Park, California, 1977.

Bray, Warwick, *Everyday Life of the Aztecs.* B. T. Batsford Ltd., London, and G. P. Putnam's Sons, New York, 1968.

Brenner, A., and Leighton, George R., *The Wind that Swept Mexico.* University of Texas Press, Austin and London, 1971.

Brosnahan, Tom, and Kretchman, Jane, *Mexico and Guatemala on 10 dollars a day.* Arthur Frommer Inc., New York, 1977.

Burland, Cottie, and Forman, Werner, *Feathered Serpent and Smoking Mirror: Gods and Fate in Ancient Mexico.* Orbis Publishing Ltd., London, 1975.

Calvert, Peter, *Mexico.* Ernest Benn Ltd., London, 1973.

Calvert, Peter, *The Mexicans, How They Live and Work.* David & Charles Ltd., Newton Abbot, 1975.

Casasola, Gustavo, *Historia Grafica de la Revolucion Mexicana.* Editorial F. Trillas, S.A., Mexico, 1965.

Cline, Howard F., *Mexico: Revolution to Evolution 1940-60.* Oxford University Press, London, New York, Toronto, 1962.

Collis, Maurice, *Cortes and Montezuma.* Faber & Faber Ltd., London, 1954.

Conkling, A. R., *Appletons' Guide to Mexico.* D. Appleton Co., New York, 1884.

Cornelius, Wayne A., *Politics and the Migrant Poor in Mexico City.* Stanford University Press, California, 1975.

Cumberland, Charles C., *Mexican Revolution, Genesis under Madero.* University of Texas Press, Austin, 1952.

Denison Ross, E., and Power, Eileen, eds., *Bernal Díaz del Castillo. The Discovery and Conquest of Mexico 1517-1521.* George Routledge & Sons Ltd., London, 1928.

Eckstein, Susan, *The Poverty of Revolution. The State and the Urban Poor in Mexico.*

Princeton University Press, Princeton, New Jersey, 1977.

Editions Berlitz, *Berlitz Travel Guide, Mexico City.* Macmillan S.A., Switzerland, 1978.

Fuentes, Patricia de, *The Conquistadors.* The Orion Press, New York, 1963.

Greene, Graham, *The Lawless Roads.* Penguin Books Ltd., London, 1947.

Grieb, Kenneth J., *The United States and Huerta.* University of Nebraska Press, Lincoln, 1969.

Hagen, Victor Wolfgang von, *The Aztec: Man and Tribe.* The New American Library, New York, London, Scarborough, Ontario, 1961.

Haslip, Joan, *The Crown of Mexico.* Holt, Rinehart & Winston Inc., New York, 1971.

Hepburn, Andrew, *Rand McNally Guide to Mexico.* Rand McNally & Co., Chicago, New York, San Francisco, 1971.

Innes, Hammond, *The Conquistadors.* William Collins, Sons & Co. Ltd., London, Glasgow, 1969.

Lewis, Oscar, *Five Families.* Basic Books Inc., New York, 1959.

Lewis, Oscar, *The Children of Sánchez.* Penguin Books Ltd., Harmondsworth, Middlesex, 1961.

Lowry, Malcolm, *Under the Volcano.* Penguin Books Ltd., Harmondsworth, Middlesex, 1969.

Martinez, Orlando, *The Great Landgrab: The Mexican-American War 1846-1848.* Quartet Books Ltd., London, 1975.

Nagel Publishers, *Nagel's Encyclopedia-Guide, Mexico.* Geneva, 1974.

Newton, Norman, *Thomas Gage in Spanish America.* Faber & Faber Ltd., London, 1969.

Nicholson, Irene, *The X in Mexico.* Faber & Faber Ltd., London, 1965.

Payne, Robert, *Mexico City.* Harcourt, Brace & World Inc., New York, 1968.

Peterson, Frederick, *Ancient Mexico.* Capricorn Books, New York, 1959.

Prescott, William H., *History of the Conquest of Mexico.* Swan Sonnenschein & Co., London, 1890.

Ramirez, Pedro, et al., *Mexico: Art, Architecture, Archaeology, Ethnography. The National Museum of Anthropology.* Harry N.

Abrams Inc., New York, in association with Helvetica Press, Inc., 1968.

Ramos, Samuel, *Profile of Man and Culture in Mexico.* University of Texas Press, Austin, 1962.

Robertson, Donald, *Mexican Manuscript Painting of the Early Colonial Period.* Yale University Press, New Haven, 1959.

Rodriguez, Antonio, *A History of Mexican Mural Painting.* Thames & Hudson Ltd., London, 1967.

Rojas, Pedro, *The Art and Architecture of Mexico.* Hamlyn Publishing Group Ltd., Feltham, Middlesex, 1968.

Scott, Robert E., *Mexican Government in Transition.* University of Illinois Press, Urbana, 1959.

Selby, John, *The Eagle and the Serpent. The Invasions of Mexico: 1519 and 1846.* Hamish Hamilton Ltd., London, 1978.

Serocold, John, *Oil in Mexico.* Chapman & Hall Ltd., London, 1938.

Simon, Kate, *Mexico: Places and Pleasures.* The World Publishing Company, Cleveland and New York, 1963.

Simpson, Leslie Byrd, *Many Mexicos.* University of California Press, Berkeley and Los Angeles, 1964.

Smith, Bradley, *Mexico. A History in Art.* Phaidon Press Ltd., London, 1975.

Soustelle, Jacques, *The Daily Life of the Aztecs on the Eve of the Spanish Conquest.* George Weidenfeld & Nicolson Ltd., London, 1961.

Tannenbaum, Frank, *Mexico. The Struggle for Peace and Bread.* Alfred A. Knopf, New York, 1960.

Toussaint, Manuel, *Colonial Art in Mexico.* University of Texas Press, Austin and London, 1967.

Turner, John Kenneth, *Barbarous Mexico.* Cassell & Co. Ltd., London, New York, Toronto and Melbourne, 1911.

Vernon, Raymond, *The Dilemma of Mexico's Development.* Harvard University Press, Cambridge, Massachusetts, 1963.

Weil, Thomas E., *Area Handbook for Mexico.* U.S. Government Printing Office, Washington, D.C., 1975.

Acknowledgements and Picture Credits

The editors wish to thank the following for their valuable assistance: Elizabeth Baquedano de Alvarez, London; Roberto and Guadalupe Donadi, Mexico City; William Donaldson, London; Tim Fraser, London; Rosemary Helfer, London; Lilia O. de Hidalgo, Mexico City; Julio Lara, Mexico City; The London Library, St. James's Square, London; Dr. Norman Long, University of Durham; Mexican Embassy, London; Mexican National Tourist Council, London; Russell Miller, London; Beejay Moffatt, London; Winona O'Connor, London; Nigel Parkinson, Mexico City; Susan de la Plain, London; Armando Ramirez, Mexico City; Dr. Bryan Roberts, University of Manchester; Dr. Mauricio Garcia and Angela Sainz, Mexico City; Marie-Rose Séguy, Bibliothèque Nationale, Paris; Jasmine Spencer, London; Dr. Guy Thomson, University of Warwick; Linda Ulrich-Sutherland, St. Gallen, Switzerland; Giles Wordsworth, London.

Pages 181 and 187, song, *"Despierta!"* reproduced by courtesy of Maestro Gabriel Ruiz and Maestro Gabriel Luna de la Fuente. Quotations on page 25 from *The Labyrinth of Solitude* by Octavio Paz, translated by Lysander Kemp, published by Allen Lane, Penguin Press, 1967, reproduced by permission of Penguin Books Ltd., and Grove Press, Inc. © 1961. Quotation on page 37 from *The Conquest of New Spain* by Bernal Díaz, translated by J. M. Cohen (Penguin Classics, 1963) © J. M. Cohen, 1963, reproduced by permission of Penguin Books Ltd. Quotation on page 46 from *Everyday Life of the Aztecs* by Warwick Bray, reproduced by permission of B. T. Batsford Ltd., London, and G. P. Putnam's Sons, New York. Quotation on page 48 from *The Discovery and Conquest of Mexico* by Bernal Díaz del Castillo, translated by A. P. Maudslay, 1928, reproduced by permission of Routledge & Kegan Paul Ltd. © 1956 by Farrar, Straus and

Cudahy (now Farrar, Straus & Giroux, Inc.).

Sources for pictures in this book are shown below. Credits for the pictures from left to right are separated by commas; from top to bottom by dashes.

All photographs are by Harald Sund except: Pages 12, 13—Map by Hunting Surveys Ltd., London (Silhouettes by Anna Pugh). 39—Uppsala, University Library. 44, 45—Archives de Documentation Photographique Cauboue. Courtesy Division Manuscrits Orientaux, Bibliothèque Nationale, Paris. 49—Ferdinand Anton. 53—Copyright: Bradley Smith. Courtesy Museo Nacional de Historia, Mexico City. 110, 111—Culver Pictures. Archivo Casasola INAH. 115—Associated Press, London. 124 to 133—Archivo Casasola INAH, except 128 (inset left)—The Bettman Archive.

Index

Numerals in italics indicate a photograph or drawing of the subject mentioned.

Colour reproduction by Irwin Photography Ltd., at their Leeds Studio.
Filmsetting by C. E. Dawkins (Typesetters) Ltd., London, SE1 1UN.
Printed and bound in Italy by Arnoldo Mondadori, Verona.